The Lady in the Tower

Reason Leading Secular Women into the City of Ladies
BRITISH LIBRARY, HARLEY MS 4431, FOL. 323

The Lady in the Tower

Medieval Courtesy Literature
for Women

Diane Bornstein

ARCHON BOOKS
1983

First published 1983 as an Archon Book,
an imprint of
The Shoe String Press, Inc.
Hamden, Connecticut 06514

Printed in the United States of America

Library of Congress Cataloging in Publication Data
Bornstein, Diane, [date]
   The lady in the tower
   Bibliography: p.
   Includes index.
   1. Women—History—Middle Ages, 500-1500.
2. Women in literature—History—Middle Ages, 500-1500.
3. Courtesy in literature—History—Middle Ages, 500-
1500.   4. Didactic literature—History—Middle Ages,
500-1500.   I. Title.
HQ1143.B67   1983   305.4'09'02   82-20649
ISBN 0-208-01995-2

Contents

Acknowledgments

A large part of this book was written while I was on a fellowship from the National Endowment for the Humanities, and it was supported also by a grant from the Research Foundation of the City University of New York. I wish to express my deepest gratitude to these organizations for their aid. I am greatly indebted to Richard R. Griffith, Carleton W. Carroll, Robert P. Miller, Gary F. Waller, Joan Ferrante, and Carole Levin for their reading of the manuscript and their many helpful suggestions. I am especially thankful to Carleton W. Carroll for his careful proofreading of the manuscript.

I

Images of Women in Medieval Literature
versus
Images in the Courtesy Books

The popular image of a medieval woman is a lady in a tower wearing a pointed headdress, a flowing cloak, and a sumptuous gown of silk, velvet, or cloth of gold; she is gazing out the window at knights riding to a tournament, or at peasants laboring in the field. This picture captures the popular imagination because it represents the romantic, chivalric ideas about women that developed during the Middle Ages. Nevertheless, it owes more to medieval romances than to the social life of the time, or even to the more realistic didactic literature written for and about women.

In the typical romance, little attention is given to the characterization of the lady, who exists mainly as a motivating force or source of inspiration for the knight. As such, she must be an image of ideal beauty. She is usually portrayed as a young woman with long blond hair, grey-blue eyes, a small red mouth, a red and white complexion, and a slim body. Emelye in Chaucer's Knight's Tale is an example of the courtly romance heroine. As soon as Palamon and Arcite observe her, they fall in love, which ends their brotherhood in arms and begins the contest that provides a plot for the rest of the romance. Yet Emelye is never realized as a character. She never speaks to either of the two men, is totally unaware of their love for her or even of their existence, and remains only an image in their minds and in the mind of the reader. We do not meet her again until the pre-tournament scene at the temple of Diana, where she prays to Diana to preserve her virginity and to keep both men away from her.[1] Chaucer treats the theme of the distant lady comically, exaggerating the situation, but this type of heroine is common in medieval romance. The medieval heroine may be a temptress or a virgin, disdainful or unaware, but she rarely plays an active role. Since her main function is to provide motivation for male characters, we usually see her through their eyes.

In the courtly lyric, the lady looks the same but is even less of a real human being. Courtly literature is concerned with the effect of love on a man, his development of self-awareness and the ensuing conflicts. The woman whom the poet loves is a mirror in which he sees his ideal self. How he sees her depends on how he feels about himself or how he thinks she is treating him.[2] Whether she is portrayed as a saint or a devil, a virgin or a whore, depends more on the man's feelings than on the woman's character.

Women are presented entirely as symbols of abstract qualities or psychological states in allegories. Abstractions such as the Virtues were personified as women in classical art and literature, and this practice was continued in the Middle Ages. Sometimes a classical personification was identified as female merely because the abstract noun it represented was feminine in gender.[3] Once a concept was identified as feminine, its feminine attributes tended to be emphasized. For example, in commenting on the figure of Philosophy in Boethius's *Consolation of Philosophy*, Guillaume de Conches tells us that she appears as a woman because she softens the ferocity of souls, nourishes children with her milk, is accustomed to tending the sick, and the noun *philosophy* is feminine in Greek.[4] Medieval personification thus combined grammatical literalism, physiological realism, and psychological symbolism.

In medieval allegory, undesirable qualities are often personified as ugly old women, whereas desirable ones are beautiful young girls. In the *Romance of the Rose*, Hatred is an ugly, filthy old woman. Felony and Villainy have a similar appearance. Avarice is dirty, skinny, discolored, and old. Sorrow is pale, gaunt, and old. Old Age is decrepit, wrinkled, toothless, and shrunken. On the other hand, Idleness, the porter to the gate of the garden of love, is a beautiful young blonde with a well-proportioned body. Joy and Courtesy are also beautiful young ladies.[5] There is an identification of good qualities with feminine youth and beauty, and bad qualities with feminine old age. Old women are almost always described as repulsive in medieval literature.

The repulsive old woman also appears as a stereotype in antifeminist literature. She is usually a cursing, scolding, sexually aggressive, hefty old virago who is after a husband, or making life miserable for the one she has, or taking revenge upon men. La Vieille, the Duenna in the *Romance of the Rose*, is representative of this type. When she was young, she made men give her gifts, fight over her, and even kill themselves for love. All of her beauty and skills were used to entrap and deceive men and to enrich herself. When we meet her as a character in the *Romance of the Rose*, she is wrinkled, ugly, old, and no longer able to seduce men.[6]

Chaucer modeled his Wife of Bath on La Vieille, but made her more likeable and provided more particulars about her "wandrynge by the way."[7] The Wife is a skilled businesswoman involved in the clothmaking trade, but that is where her economic productivity ends. She spends money prodigally on her flashy clothes. The red color of her coverchiefs, stockings, and complexion symbolizes her unrestrained sexuality. Dressed in her gay scarlet gown, she goes to vigils, processions, church events, miracle plays, weddings, and on pilgrimages to show off her finery and to seek friends and lovers. She argues, curses, scolds, plots, and gossips behind her husband's back, using all her wits to gain *maistrie* in her marriage. The Wife's arts of trickery enabled her to gain the dominant role in all five of her marriages; when we meet her on the pilgrimage to Canterbury, she is well into middle age but still able to attract men.

Although medieval satire is sometimes described as realistic, the portraits of sexually aggressive, cursing, scolding women that we find in antifeminist literature are just as unrealistic as the ones of passive golden ladies that we find in courtly romances and lyrics. These portraits reveal more about the fantasies, dreams, and nightmares of men than they do about the lives of women. We can discover something about the lives of women, as opposed to images created for romantic or satirical purposes, in the courtesy literature of the time. I am defining courtesy literature broadly as didactic literature meant to serve as a guide for secular life. My definition would include not only books of etiquette, but also books of advice from mother or father to daughter, books of instruction addressed to women by clerks, mirrors for the princess, and even *Arts of Love* containing practical advice that was meant to be taken seriously. The authors include fathers, mothers, husbands, priests, court poets, and scholars. Although most of them remain anonymous, a few, such as Saint Louis, were famous historical personalities. Since most of the authors were men, we usually get men's ideas of what women should have been doing. Nevertheless, these images are more realistic than those in other kinds of literature. A knight such as Geoffrey de la Tour-Landry may have written love poems and romances in his youth, but when he wrote a book of instruction for his daughters, he was more concerned about their frugality and morality than their beauty. When a knight addressed his real wife or daughter rather than his ideal lady, he was most interested in her role as a household manager. Different groups of men did not always agree about what roles and activities were proper for women. The Church Fathers thought they should pray and be chaste. The troubadours thought they should cultivate their beauty, read poetry, and flirt. Almost everyone thought they should marry, have children, and be efficient household managers. Most of the courtesy books emphasize woman's familial roles and claim her place to be within the home.

Although some of the anonymous works purport to be written by women, the only known woman author of courtesy books before 1500 was Christine de Pizan. Her works are particularly important because we are able to envision the lives and problems of medieval women through the words of a woman. Because of her varied experience, she was uniquely qualified to comment on the lives of medieval women. She received an education that was normally given only to boys. Under the supervision of her scholar-father, she studied Latin, literature, various sciences, and philosophy. Married at fifteen and widowed at twenty-five, with three children and a mother to support, she put her education to good use to become France's first professional woman writer. Christine has earned a reputation as the first feminist. Nevertheless, her views are moderate enough to represent the general opinion of the time. In the works of Christine, we can see how an intelligent, educated woman responded to the feminine ideal of her time, mainly a creation of the male establishment. Sometimes she internalized the attitudes of her male-dominated society. At other times she came to the same conclusions for different reasons. For example, she praised chastity not for the sake of physical purity, but because it frees women from the domination of men. Frequently, she questioned the traditional view or presented one of her own. In the *Cité des dames*, she used the dialogue form to raise questions about women's lack of power. She was the only author to portray the full range of women's political, economic, social, and sexual roles in medieval society, from the princess to the prostitute.

The courtesy books were meant to serve as a guide for behavior in the real world. Consequently, they reveal a great deal about the roles women were expected to play in the Middle Ages, the restrictions they were supposed to observe, and the responsibilities they had to fulfill. The frequent admonitions and some of the anecdotes offer glimpses of unsanctioned behavior. Of course, the images presented in the courtesy books are not always realistic but are sometimes idealized in their own way. The authors often had a polemical purpose and would exaggerate to convince women of the value of a particular way of life. For instance, a number of the authors of treatises on virginity made motherhood seem repulsive. In poems by the troubadours, flirtation is idealized as *fin amor* (fine love), whereas in treatises by clerks it is condemned as the gateway to adultery. Writers sometimes ignored or criticized a development of their time rather than report it, such as the increasing economic role of women. At times the courtesy books reflect their age, and at times they resist it. Yet even when they resist it, they illuminate the mental climate, the *sens intellectuel* of the period. They are one of the most valuable sources available for information about the lives of women and, more particularly, attitudes toward them.

The courtesy books were most popular during the high Middle Ages when various factors combined to give them a strong appeal: the encyclopedic impulse to classify and define, the insistence upon hierarchy in political and social theory, the actual social mobility and instability of the time, the attempt of the aristocracy to affirm their position, and the rise of the middle class. Most of the courtesy books were written between the late twelfth and the fifteenth centuries. (My cut-off date is 1500, since significant changes in attitudes occur in the sixteenth century, particularly in regard to the education of women.) Many were written in France. As in other areas of medieval literature and culture, the example of France dominated other countries. Some were written in England, Germany, Italy, and Spain, but the differences from country to country were slight. The medieval ideal of the lady was just as universal as the ideal of the knight.[8] Since many of the treatises repeat the same information, I have focused upon the most important works and have organized my material according to the roles of women, as set forth in the courtesy books. Summaries have been provided since most of the books are not readily available. I have analyzed them from the point of view of a medieval scholar studying the connections between life and didactic literature, and also from that of a twentieth-century woman seeking the origins of ideas about women that have dominated Western culture.

II

Woman as Virgin

The earliest didactic treatises composed for women were those of the Church Fathers. They were written long before the period upon which we are focusing, but they were important sources that set the tone for many medieval works. The Church Fathers exalted the ideals of asceticism and virginity, and criticized marriage, believing that a carnal union interfered with the life of the spirit. The elevation of virginity and the spiritual life coincided with a derogation of the life-bearing function of women. Young girls were exhorted to remain virgins. Widows were urged not to remarry. Women were praised most highly when they renounced their biological and sexual role.

While exalting virginity, the Church Fathers criticized women's beauty, seeing it as an enticement to lust. They urged women not to improve their appearance and condemned artificial means of enhancing beauty, such as using makeup or tinting hair, as an insult to God the Creator. If a woman had natural beauty, she was exhorted to hide it so as not to tempt men. In *De cultu feminarum*, Tertullian states that women serve as the "gate of the devil" when they enhance their beauty to attract men.[1] Women should not wear jewels, ornaments, luxurious clothing, makeup, or elaborate coiffures, nor tint their hair. Artificial methods of enhancing beauty please the devil rather than God. As temples of the Lord, women should not change their appearance and should be models of chastity. The good Christian woman who adorns herself with virtues, remains subject to her husband, stays within her house, and occupies her hands with the distaff and spindle is a valuable partner in marriage.

Although Tertullian had some words of praise for marriage and was married himself, he believed it was better to remain a virgin because virginity allowed a person to turn all his or her attention to God. In accordance with his positive feelings about chastity, he disapproved of second marriages, and advised his own wife not to remarry if he should die first. The asceticism of Tertullian strongly influenced later Church Fathers. His praise of marriage was neglected, but his criticism of women who adorn themselves, his praise of virginity or widowhood, and his negative attitude toward procreation were continued.[2]

The most important authorities for later medieval writers were Ambrose, Jerome, and Augustine. Ambrose, Bishop of Milan, preached and wrote on the virginal life throughout his episcopate. He had a more positive view of women than many of the Church Fathers, seeing the feminine as a principle in mankind that extended beyond the social or physical boundaries of the female sex. Within mankind, woman represents the principle of universality and life.[3] Yet in spite of his positive views about women and their reproductive function, Ambrose still saw virginity as superior to marriage. By freeing a person from bondage to another human being, virginity manifests the equality of male and female as souls. For Ambrose, the soul is nonsexual.[4] Virginity releases men and women from the physical bonds of sex and allows them to realize their underlying equality of spirit as human beings. Ambrose eulogizes virginity in *De virginibus ad Marcellinam sororem suam*, a work written for his older sister Marcellina, who had been consecrated to God as a virgin when she was a young girl.[5]

Not all virgins or nuns upheld the high ideals of their order. As a bishop, Ambrose was concerned with such lapses of discipline. His *Ad virginem devotam exhortatio* probably was written for some nuns who had been negligent in following the rules of their order.[6] They had been consecrated to God and were the spouses of Christ. Why did they seek the company of men? He warns them about the corruption of men and tells them to flee from them. They should destroy all worldly desires in themselves, remain pure in body and spirit, and not seek worldly comforts, such as a soft bed. They should pray, give alms, fast, visit the sick, avoid the vices of anger and swearing, and practice the virtue of humility.[7] The rules of behavior emphasized by Ambrose suggest the abuses committed by the nuns: flirting, seeking physical comforts, neglecting religious duties, and arguing. Since he was criticizing abuses, this treatise has an inflammatory tone. On the whole, Ambrose's works are characterized by tolerance and moderation. He had a positive attitude toward women and praised virginity without condemning marriage and motherhood.

One of the most enthusiastic proponents of virginity and the monastic life was Jerome, friend and student of Ambrose. He saw women as inferior but believed a woman could rise above her nature through virginity and the study of scripture. He treated women who chose such a life as equals, giving them advice, instruction, and encouragement. While he was living in Rome, he found a number of disciples among a group of Christian women who had assembled together to lead an ascetic life. Their leader was Marcella, a noble, rich, childless widow. She had met Athanasius, Bishop of Alexandria, when she was a child and was deeply impressed by his tales of Christian hermits and mystics who lived in the deserts of Syria and Egypt. When her husband died, she decided to lead an ascetic life of prayer and study, and gathered around her a group of like-minded women. One of them was Ambrose's sister, Marcellina. The most famous member of her circle was Paula, heiress of the noble Aemilian family. Her husband had been a pagan, and she had lived the usual life of a wealthy Roman matron of high rank. After her husband's death, she turned to an ascetic life of prayer and study, and spent so much money on charity that she was criticized for squandering her children's inheritance. Her daughters Eustochium and Blesilla also joined Marcella's community. These women assembled at Marcella's palace on the Aventine Mount where they lived together, fasted, prayed, and studied. Jerome met with them as their instructor.[8]

Jerome wrote a number of treatises on virginity for these disciples. The *Epistola ad Eustochium de custodia virginitatis* was written for Eustochium, Paula's third daughter, who had wished to take the veil from the time she was a child. Jerome praises the life of virginity chosen by Eustochium. He briefly enumerates the disadvantages of marriage, using the rhetorical trick of claiming he is not going to state them.

> I am writing this to you, Lady Eustochium (I am bound to call my Lord's bride "lady"), that from the very beginning

of my discourse you may learn that I do not today intend
to sing the praises of the virginity which you have adopted
and proved to be so good. Nor shall I now reckon up the
disadvantages of marriage, such as pregnancy, a crying
baby, the tortures of jealousy, the cares of household management, and the cutting short by death of all its fancied
blessings.[9]

Jerome always speaks of motherhood in negative terms. He discusses
the temptations of the flesh that assail a virgin. Saint Paul himself
could not trust his body. One must keep watch over the flesh and
the spirit. Even if a virgin's upbringing has accustomed her to opu-
lence (and this was true of many of his women disciples), she should
be content with a simple diet and plain clothing. She should avoid
the company of worldly women and women of bad reputation.

Jerome's *Ad Laetam de institutione filiae* is a letter of advice
regarding the education of a girl who was consecrated as a virgin.
Laeta was the wife of Toxotius, son of Paula. They had consecrated
their daughter as a virgin before she was born and named her Paula
after her grandmother. He recommends an unworldly, cloistered,
studious upbringing for the child. She should learn to read and write
at a young age. His description of how she should be taught shows a
good understanding of a child's nature:

Have a set of letters made for her, of boxwood or of ivory,
and tell her their names. Let her play with them, making
play a road to learning, and let her not only grasp the
right order of the letters and remember their names in a
simple song, but also frequently upset their order and mix
the last letters with the middle ones, the middle with the
first. Thus she will know them all by sight as well as by
sound. When she begins with uncertain hand to use the
pen, either let another hand be put over hers to guide her
baby fingers, or else have the letters marked on the tablet
so that her writing may follow their outlines and keep to
their limits without straying away. Offer her prizes for
spelling, tempting her with such trifling gifts as please
young children. Let her have companions too in her lessons, so that she may seek to rival them and be stimulated
by any praise they win. You must not scold her if she is

somewhat slow; praise is the best sharpener of wits. Let her be glad when she is first and sorry when she falls behind. Above all take care not to make her lessons distasteful; a childish dislike often lasts longer than childhood. [10]

For someone who ranted so much about the cares of raising children, Jerome shows a surprising tenderness toward young Paula. He even offers to be her tutor and foster father if Laeta sends her to her grandmother's convent in Bethlehem, which she eventually did.

Jerome recommends an ambitious program of study for young Paula. She should recite the scriptures in Greek and Latin every day, being careful to use the correct pronunciation. Her study of the Bible should begin with the Psalms. She should then learn lessons of life from the Book of Proverbs, which will teach her to despise the things of this world. The Book of Job will teach her patience. She should then move on to the Gospels, the Acts of the Apostles, and the Epistles. In studying the Old Testament, she should read the Prophets, the Heptateuch, Kings, Chronicles, the Book of Ezra, and the Book of Esther. Finally, she may read the Song of Songs, which she will be able to interpret spiritually in view of her earlier study. Jerome also recommends treatises by Cyprian, Athanasius, and Hilary.

In addition to studying, she should learn to use the distaff and spindle. Her nurse, teachers, and companions must be chosen very carefully. She should not attend the receptions of her parents and should go out as little as possible, except to church. She should not listen to music, except for the singing of psalms and hymns. She should not drink wine, unless a little is needed for her health; should eat plain but nourishing food, and dress simply, without jewels or ornaments. Instead of jewels or silks, she should love the manuscripts of Holy Scriptures.

For Jerome, virginity was the only state worthy of praise. He praised marriage only because it produced virgins. Since marriage and fruitfulness came after the Fall, he believed they were more of a curse than a blessing. Under the old law, the fruitful married woman was praised more than the virgin; under the new law, the reverse is true. He cites Tertullian and Ambrose to support his point of view but actually goes further than those authorities in extolling virginity and criticizing marriage. [11]

Saint Augustine had a more moderate attitude toward virginity and marriage. He did not approve of encomiums of virginity that discouraged Christians from marrying. Nevertheless, he still saw virginity as a superior state. In the hierarchy of roles that could be realized by a woman, that of the unmarried girl who expects to marry ranks lowest. She is worried about how to please her future husband and how to raise her children without knowing who that husband will be and without yet having any children. The married woman comes next. She is no longer in a state of uncertainty but is divided between her religious and secular duties. The virgin ranks highest since she can devote herself to God.[12]

Under the influence of the Church Fathers, clerics continued to write treatises in praise of virginity throughout the Middle Ages. Among the most interesting are works addressed to nuns, for they reveal something about the lives of women within the convents. The earliest convent was founded in 512 by Bishop Caesarius of Arles and was headed by his sister Caesaria.[13] He wrote for it the first set of conventual rules for women, the *Regula ad virgines* (513), and also wrote two letters of instruction for his sister to offer her guidance in her role as abbess.[14] He tells her to give precedence to spiritual thoughts but to care for her health and that of the nuns who are entrusted to her. She should always set a good example for the sisters, being the first to begin working and the last to stop, and fast along with the others so they cannot accuse her of preaching abstinence with a full stomach. She should not be more elegant than the others in her dress, but should outdo them in virtuous manners. She should treat all of the sisters with justice, moderation, charity, and mercy, not showing favoritism to any. When she needs advice, she should consult the oldest sisters. When she has to confer with the outside world, she should first commend her soul to God. She should be known from afar by her reputation and good deeds but not be seen in public too often. Caesarius's *Epistola hortatoria ad virginem Deo dedicatem* is a letter in praise of virginity very similar to those written by the Church Fathers.[15]

Aldhelm, the seventh-century Anglo-Saxon scholar who became abbot of Malmesbury and bishop of Sherborne, wrote a treatise for the nuns at Barking entitled *De laudibus virginitatis sive de virginate sanctorum*.[16] He praises the virtues of the sisters and compares them to gymnosophists or honey bees, who gather knowledge from everywhere. They study not only the Bible, but also history, grammar, orthography, and metrics. They also resemble bees in their obedience and chastity. He praises virginity as the superior way of life but states that one should not condemn marriage. Virgins should not become proud, for pride is the worst of sins. Virginity alone is not enough; it must be supported by other virtues. Aldhelm differs from many writers in not placing undue value on virginity alone. The sisters should follow the example of the ascetics of the Old and New Testament, the virgins, and the martyrs. Attacking the pomp and vanity of the time, he exhorts them to renounce luxury. In conclusion, he states that if the first treatise pleases his audience, he will celebrate virginity in verse. This he does in his *De laudibus virginum*, which contains nothing new in content.[17] Aldhelm's treatise reveals the high level of learning attained by nuns in seventh-century England. It is characterized by a balanced attitude toward chastity as only one of a woman's virtues rather than as the entire foundation for her honor, and by a lenient outlook on marriage.

An extremely intolerant attitude toward marriage is found in *Hali Meidenhad*, a homily written in a West Midland dialect in the early thirteenth century.[18] The anonymous author attacks marriage and glorifies virginity most vehemently. He states that from her elevated state as the bride of Christ, the virgin looks down upon married women, who are thralls to the flesh. Although the virgin's body dwells on earth, it is as if her spirit dwelled in heaven, free from all worldly vexations. By contrast, the married woman leads a life of slavery. Her husband will turn her into a household drudge, give her innumerable troubles, and make her endure vexation, anger, and shame for very poor hire in the end.

Living at a time when people favored marriage and were sentimental about family life, Oswald Cockayne, the Victorian editor of *Hali Meidenhad*, was apparently outraged by the author's attacks on marriage and the coarse passages in the work. Although he had too much scholarly integrity to bowdlerize these passages, he translated them into Latin in his Modern English version. For example, the following description of sexual intercourse made the editor resort to Latin.

That most unpleasant burning of the flesh, that burning itch of bodily lust, before that loathsome work, that beastly coming together, that shameless summoning, that filthy, stinking, dishonorable deed.[19]

The author describes how the husband will mistreat his wife:

> While he is at home, thy wide walls seem too narrow for thee; his looking on thee makes thee aghast; his loathsome voice and his rude grumbling fill thee with horror. He chideth and jaweth thee, and he insults thee shamefully; he maketh mock at thee, as a lecher with his hore; he beateth thee and mawleth thee as his bought thrall and patrimonial slave. Thy bones ake, and thy flesh smarteth, thy heart within thee swelleth of sore rage, and thy face externally burneth with vexation.[20]

The author describes in revolting detail the pain and sickness of pregnancy, and the manner in which a woman's body becomes ugly and distorted. This is the point of view of a life-denying male who sees pregnancy from the outside as a purely negative experience. He has no sense of the pride and pleasure a woman might feel from her awareness of the child's development within her body. Moreover, his view of pregnancy as ugly is culturally determined. Cultures that exalt fertility see a woman's pregnant body as beautiful and as an object of worship.

> Consider we what joy ariseth from gestation of children, when the offspring in thee quickeneth and groweth. How many miseries immediately wake up therewith, and work thee woe enough, fight at thine own flesh, and with many sorrows make war upon thine own nature. Thy ruddy face shall turn lean and grow green as grass. Thine eyes shall be dusky, and under them be spots, and by the giddiness of thy brain thy head shall ake sorely. Within thy belly the uterus shall swell and strut out like a water bag; thy bowels shall have pains, and there shall be stitches in thy flank, and pain rife in thy loins, heaviness in every limb. Thy breasts shall be a burthen on thy paps, and the milk in drops which trickle out of them. All thy beauty is overthrown with a withering. Thy mouth is bitter, and rolls over all that thou chewest, and with disgust accepts

whatever meat it can; that is, with want of appetite, throws it up again.[21]

Once a woman has a child, she will feel a great deal of anxiety about him, and her husband will compete for attention. The author describes the harried housewife who is trying to take care of her child, husband, cooking, and household pets all at the same time.

> And what if I ask besides, that it may seem odious, how the wife stands, that heareth when she cometh in her child scream, sees the cat at the flitch, and the hound at the hide; her cake is burning on the stone hearth, and her calf is sucking all the milk up, the earthen pot is running into the fire, and the churl is scolding. Though it be an odious tale, it ought, maiden, to deter thee more strongly from marriage, for it seems not easy to her that trieth it.[22]

Among all of the antimatrimonial works addressed to virgins, *Hali Meidenhad* paints the most miserable picture of marriage. The manuscript containing *Hali Meidenhad* also includes *Sawles Warde*, a religious allegory based on *De Anima* by Hugh of Saint Victor, as well as *Saint Katherine, Saint Margaret,* and *Saint Juliana*, tales that celebrate the lives of virgin martyrs. Since these martyrs are also used as exempla in *Hali Meidenhad*, it is possible that the works were written by the same author. The audience for the manuscript is not known, but it is likely to have been a community of nuns or anchoresses because of the emphasis on virginity and the antimatrimonial propaganda.

The audience is known for the *Ancrene Riwle*, a work also written in the West Midland dialect in the early thirteenth century.[23] Manuscripts survive in English, French, and Latin, but the original was probably in English. It was written by an anonymous priest for three young sisters of Dorset who were preparing to live the cloistered life of anchoresses. The author states that every rule has two parts: the internal, which deals with the spirit, and the external, which deals with the body. He has divided his book into eight parts: seven dealing with the inner rule, and one dealing with the outer rule. The first seven sections contain mainly religious material; the last one contains material that falls into the category of the courtesy book. I will briefly summarize all eight sections to give an idea of the rule of life the author prescribes for the three girls but will analyze chapter eight in greater detail.

Chapter one deals with devotions and gives directions for prayers on regular days, Sundays, and holidays. This chapter is entirely religious. Chapter two concerns the custody of the senses. Each sense is dealt with separately. The author states that the eyes are the gate to the heart and must be guarded with particular care. The girls should have small windows in their house, covered with black curtains containing a white cross. No man should see them without special permission. The author reserves his discussion of taste for the section on food in chapter eight and discusses speech instead. Since conversation can lead to temptation, the girls should speak as little as possible. They should make the sign of the cross before receiving visitors and make the visit as brief as possible. They should confess to a good priest but avoid and distrust bad ones. Even when making confession, they should not be alone with the priest but should have someone else in the house. The author did not trust men to be alone with the girls, not even priests. This makes sense since they would have been less protected than women in a convent. Silence should be observed at meal times and for an entire day at least once a week. They should never indulge in gossip or idle conversation, should not listen to evil words, and should avoid lying, backbiting, and flattery. They should not trust their sense of smell since often a good thing has a bad smell, or vice versa. Since touch extends all over the body, it is particularly important to keep watch over this sense. They should not embrace or touch any man, for this can awaken sinful desires. They should remember that the more the senses are scattered over external things, the less they can function inwardly.

Chapter three concerns the regulation of the inward feelings and provides reasons for choosing the solitary life. Chapter four deals with temptation, Chapter five with confession, Chapter six with penance, and Chapter seven with Christian love. Once again, these chapters are entirely religious.

Chapter eight deals with external rules and provides a good idea of the life of the anchoresses. The author states that the prescriptions were meant particularly for the three sisters, who had asked him to write the book. Before taking communion, they should fast and confess to their sins. When not fasting, they should eat two meals a day. Their food should not be too rich, they should not eat meat, and they should drink moderately. Nevertheless, they should not fast on bread and water without special permission and should not fast too frequently. They should not encourage strangers to come to their house for alms and should not give alms too prodigally. Acts of charity should be performed in secret and not to obtain a reputation for generosity. They should not desire wealth, not even to give away to others, since generosity can be a form of pride. The author is particularly emphatic in warning the girls against generosity and courtesy, virtues of the aristocracy which could be faults for anchoresses. They should give food and drink to the women and children who work for them, but man servants should not eat in their presence. No man should ever sleep in their house. The author's comments about servants reveal that the girls came from a prosperous family and did not intend to give up all of their comforts in becoming anchoresses. They should not own animals, except for a cat. If they must have a cow, they should make sure she does not distract them from their religious observances. They should not buy or sell merchandise, or take care of other people's possessions since that would involve them in worldly concerns.

The ideal of dress is one of austerity and simplicity but comfort. Their clothes should be simple, warm, and well made. The color is not important since they will rarely be seen. They should have a sufficient number of garments for day and night. Undergarments should be of a coarse material, such as flax or worsted, but they should not wear anything too rough, such as a hairshirt. They should not flagellate themselves. The author's ideal of asceticism is moderate; he does not believe in torturing the body or damaging its health. They should sleep in a gown belted at the waist. Shoes should be soft, roomy, and warm. They can sleep in stockings in the winter for warmth and can go barefoot in summer. It is not necessary for them to wear wimples. They should wear warm caps with white or black veils over them. They should not wear rings, brooches, striped belts, or gloves. Their clothes should follow the style of nuns or of the poor.

They should make their own clothes, church vestments and garments for the poor, and engage in other kinds of work, always keeping busy. They should not turn their cloister into a school. If they are approached by a young girl pupil who does not want to attend school with boys, their servant can instruct her. They should neither receive nor write letters without special permission. They should wash as often as they like and cut their hair four times a year. They can be bled four times a year, but if they can do without bloodletting, that is better. If the girls are sad or depressed, they can tell stories to amuse each other.

They should have two women servants to take care of their food, one to prepare it and one to purchase provisions. Their servants should be obedient and should not gossip about them. They should have nothing to do with men and should dress plainly. Their servants were expected to follow this same rule of life to a certain extent.

Unlike many clerics who wrote treatises addressed to virgins, the author of the *Ancrene Riwle* does not disparage romantic love and motherhood. On the contrary, he uses metaphors referring to those areas of experience in speaking of the religious life. For example, in his elucidation of Christ's love for the soul, he uses an allegory of a king wooing a lady. In explaining why God tempts us, he uses the metaphor of a mother playing with her child and hiding from him.

> The sixth comfort is that Our Lord, when He allows us to be tempted, is playing with us as a mother with her darling child. She runs away from him and hides, and leaves him on his own, and he looks around for her calling "Mama! Mama!" and crying a little, and then she runs out to him quickly, her arms outspread, and she puts them around him, and kisses him, and wipes his eyes.[24]

Rather than wanting to make the girls feel disgust toward love and marriage, as the author of *Hali Meidenhad* did, he encouraged them to sublimate their sexual, romantic, and maternal impulses.

One can't help but wonder what women thought about all this preaching of virginity. Although abbesses and nuns were among the few literate women in society, none of them wrote any treatises on virginity or commentaries on them. Interesting attitudes toward virginity are revealed, however, in the works of Christine de Pizan. Christine believed that women could become stronger and more free through the practice of chastity. In her autobiographical poem,

Lavision Christine, she portrays three allegorical female figures: the Crowned Dame, who governs the political realm of France; Dame Opinion, who directs the intellectual milieu of the University; and Dame Philosophy, who rules the spiritual world. Each lady represents an ideal, personified through female characteristics. The hierarchical scale on which the three ladies are placed represents a gradual freedom from the demands of the body, carnal desire, and the whims of fortune.[25] At the bottom of the scale is the wounded, tear-stained, nursing body of the Crowned Dame. In the middle of the scale is the rainbow-colored cloud of Dame Opinion. At the top of the scale is the blinding, bodiless light of Dame Philosophy.

The ladies also represent different stages of Christine's life and her search for truth. At each juncture of her journey, the female characteristics of the ideal lady become less physically pronounced. The Crowned Dame has the vulnerable body of a natural woman. She has been attacked by men and withdraws to offer them her nursing breasts while hiding her scars under her clothing. Christine connected bad fortune with the vulnerable female body. Dame Opinion is a cloud, a colorful, bodiless substance that floats above the heads of men, entering human bodies but never becoming part of them. Dame Philosophy is a celibate abbess of a convent who cannot be seen because her light is blinding to human eyes. Each woman is successively more serene and closer to happiness as she becomes less physical and female, more bodiless and chaste.

Christine believed that women could transcend the limitations placed upon them by nature and society by practicing chastity. In her *Cité des dames*, she zealously promotes the ideal of virginity. This treatise in praise of women, composed about 1405, is based mainly on Boccaccio's *De claris mulieribus*, but Christine contributed her own structural and thematic unity.[26] This unity evolves from the work's didactic purpose, which is to demonstrate the value of chastity for women.[27] The *Cité des dames* is a hierarchy presided over by the Virgin Mary and her worthy companions, a group of about forty saints, most of them virgin martyrs celebrated in widely known legends, such as Saint Katherine and Saint Marguerite. The virgin martyrs have gained glory by repulsing the spiritual assaults and sexual advances of male opponents.

Whether she is celebrating saints or secular heroines, Christine emphasizes the quality of virginity. When describing the Amazon queens, she associates their virginity with their strength and martial prowess. She selects material from her sources to underscore the idea of virginity and the military prowess that is its concomitant. She modifies the description of the Amazon queen Penthesilea to make her a virgin by choice. In the French version of Boccaccio that Christine used, Penthesilea seeks Hector because of sexual love and the desire to have his child. In the *Cité des dames*, Penthesilea's love is made platonic; she seeks Hector merely to see him. Christine describes Penthesilea and many of her other heroines as being of such lofty character that they never condescended to have sexual relations with men. This phrase is used so often that it practically becomes formulaic.

Christine's idea of virginity is not the traditional one of the Church Fathers, which emphasizes physical purity and virginity as a superior state to widowhood and marriage. For Christine, the main point is not whether a woman has kept her maidenhead, but whether she practices chastity. Married women and widows, who are celebrated in all three parts of the *Cité des dames*, can become honorary virgins through the practice of chastity. In the *Cité des dames*, virginity is a way of transcending the traditional servitudes of household duties, childbirth, husband, and family, and of gaining access to a free life. By continually linking virginity with strength, achievement, distinction, and fame, Christine suggests that women can attain these hitherto masculine rewards by foregoing their traditional roles as wives and mothers.

Different groups and authors used the ideal of the virgin for different purposes. The Church Fathers had a negative view of human sexuality and believed that celibacy was best for both sexes. They saw female sexuality as particularly threatening and connected it with the general wantonness of woman. In the writings of the Church Fathers, we find an emphasis on woman's responsibility for the Fall, a dread of female attractiveness, a low conception of women's motives and functions, a fear of sexuality, disparagement of marriage and motherhood, and praise of virginity as the superior state.[28] This became the position of the ecclesiastical establishment, and it was reaffirmed throughout the Middle Ages.

The ecclesiastical ideal of physical purity was taken over by the aristocracy, who used it for their own ends and applied it only to women. Men were told merely to be temperate in their sexual activities. In fact, they were often proud of their sexual vigor in engendering bastards. On the other hand, women were exhorted to be as chaste as possible. Virginity was exalted for young girls, who were told to preserve their sexual purity and modesty before marriage. Chastity was exalted for wives, who were told to use sex only for procreation or to satisfy their husbands' needs and to remain absolutely faithful to their husbands. Chastity was proclaimed as the most important virtue for a woman and the foundation for her honor.

There were practical reasons for the development of a double sexual standard. As Georges Duby points out in *Medieval Marriage*, the aristocracy was interested mainly in preserving the patrimony.[29] It was of utmost importance that a wife receive only one seed, that of her husband, so that intruders issued from another man's blood would not take their place among the claimants to the ancestral inheritance. This is why the moral code of the laity rigorously condemned adultery on the part of the woman but was more lenient toward the man. The double sexual standard went along with a differentiation in moral and behavioral codes for men and women. It was fitting for men to be aggressive, but women were supposed to be humble, modest, and obedient. The same moral virtues of chastity, humility, obedience, modesty, and piety that were called for in virgins were recommended to wives. Moreover, the strict sexual ethic went along with an ascetic ideal. Even in works addressed to aristocratic women, we find attacks on wearing makeup, tinting hair, enhancing beauty by artificial means, wearing expensive clothes and jewelry, and eating rich food. By disciplining all of their senses and by looking less attractive, women were less likely to be tempted to stray sexually or to be objects of temptation. For these practical reasons, the ideal of the virgin or the chaste wife has remained influential right up to the time of modern birth control and even beyond that period. It is a powerful weapon for controlling the sexual behavior of women.

In the works of Christine de Pizan, we find a significant departure from the preceding literary and moral tradition. Women's sexuality, she believed, is not threatening; women are simply more chaste and continent by nature than men. Through the practice of chastity women can become stronger and more independent. Christine emphasizes the worldly advantages of virginity rather than the spiritual ones. The *Cité des dames* celebrates virginity as the path to achievement and fame. By not enslaving herself to a man in a sexual relationship and by foregoing the traditional roles of wife and mother, a woman can achieve distinction in the political, intellectual, spiritual, or artistic realm. The choice that Christine offers, although not stated in those terms, is actually between career and family. The author herself was not able to pursue a career as a scholar and writer until her husband had died. By remaining a widow, she could devote much of her time and attention to writing, even though she still had to fulfill her responsibilities as a mother. Her own experience would have suggested that pursuing a career and marriage were incompatible, and that celibacy fostered the life of the mind. Her attitude toward sexuality resembles that of radical feminists who see sex as a form of enslavement to a man, and who consequently advise women to be celibate or at least continent.

III

Woman as Coquette

An ideal of woman diametrically opposed to that of the virgin can be found in the works of the troubadours. Rather than condemning the beauty of women, the troubadours saw it as her most important asset and encouraged her to enhance it. Along with their worship of beauty went an aesthetic view of life, a belief in the enjoyment of secular art, music, and literature. Their aestheticism clashed with the asceticism of the Church. An even greater conflict existed between the sexual attitudes of the troubadours and those of the Church. Rather than criticizing romantic love, the troubadours praised it as the highest good in life; as a force that ennobled the individual and allowed him to realize his greatest potential. To designate the feelings and physical reactions associated with romantic love, they used the term *fin amor* (literally "fine love," as opposed to a less refined sexual passion), called "courtly love" by modern scholars. In their lyrics, the troubadours celebrated a love that was frankly extramarital. In their courtesy books, they offered a domesticated version of courtly love, giving directions for flirtation but not for adultery. Discussions of love in the courtesy books suggest that the code of courtly love did exist in the real world. It justified not adultery but rather the fantasy of adultery. It provided a source for "lines" that could be delivered sincerely or insincerely, and a framework for a game of flirtation. The main point of the game was not to get a woman into bed but to enter into a play world where the players could demonstrate their social and rhetorical skills.

Georges Duby's discussion of marital practices in twelfth-century

31

France provides a sociological explanation for the popularity of the game of courtly love.[1] In order to curb the proliferation of potential heirs and to avoid divided inheritances, the heads of households pursued increasingly restrictive matrimonial strategies. They tried to marry off all their daughters to create a widespread network of alliances. However, they wished to marry only their oldest son, unless the others could be matched with heiresses. This practice resulted in a large number of bachelors, who formed turbulent bands that roamed the country in search of adventures, wives, or the protection of a lord. There was a deep division between the bachelors, who were called "youths" (*juvenes*) no matter what their age, and the married men (*seniores*), who represented the principle of order in aristocratic society. The chivalric ideology extolled the life of adventure as a compensation for the powerlessness and frustrations of "youth."

The real aim of a *juven* was to obtain a wife, by honest or dishonest means, who would bring him stability and turn him into a *senior*. The game of courtly love allowed the *juvenes* to engage in fantasies of abduction. Their dream was carried into the very house of the patron who retained them and who went to bed every night with his own wife. The favors of their patron's wife became the stake in the competition among the bachelors of the court. The aim was a "mock capture" that derived much of its excitement from flouting the strict prohibition against adultery. The game of love expressed hostility to marriage, yet it emphasized the importance of marriage at the same time. It provided a safety valve for frustrated bachelors and chaste wives whose marriages were based on economic rather than romantic considerations. Its rules demanded that the female partner be married, and that the knight love a lady he would not be ashamed to marry. Actually, the lord of the house controlled the game, for he used these social rituals for his own ends. By exhibiting his largesse to the point of letting his lady flirt with his retainers, he was able to gain a stronger hold over the young men of his household.

In the latter part of the twelfth century, when aristocratic families came to obtain wealth from more varied sources, heads of households became more generous in providing for the marriages of younger sons.[2] At that time, the ideal of courtly love became domesticated. Aristocratic society offered an alternative to fantasies and games of abduction—the glorification of marriage.[3] The ideal of courtly love was not abandoned, however, but set within a framework of courtship and marriage. The same lines were addressed to a prospective wife, or to one's own wife, rather than to the wife of another man. The game of courtly love thus was an important social ritual, in its undomesticated and domesticated forms, and writers of the courtesy books taught their audience how to play it.

Aristocratic women were given advice on appearance, deportment, and behavior in the game of love in an *ensenhamen* (treatise of instruction) by Garin lo Brun, a knight and troubadour of Veillac who flourished during the latter part of the twelfth century.[4] Garin is not mentioned as author in either of the two extant manuscripts, but Matfre Ermengaud quotes it in the *Breviari d'amor* and identifies Garin as the author, citing him as an authority on love and courtesy.[5] The poet opens with a conventional but lively description of the return of spring with its flowering trees and singing birds. Spring makes him think of love, which has fallen into a decadent state; people are no longer interested in honor, courtesy, and loyalty but are concerned only with gain and profit. While he is brooding, an attractive noble lady appears who asks him how she should act to earn a reputation for honor and courtesy. The poet agrees to advise her, and at this point the instructional part of the *ensenhamen* begins.

Garin first offers advice on personal appearance. A lady should wash her face when she gets up in the morning. She should wear a fresh white undergarment of a soft fabric, clothes that flatter her face and figure, and shoes that make her feet appear small. All her clothing should be neat, clean, and in good order. He maids should be skilled in helping her dress and arrange her hair.

Garin next provides advice regarding deportment. A lady should walk slowly, with small steps and without tiring herself. She should walk and ride gracefully. When going to church, she should be accompanied by people with whom she is not ashamed to be seen. She should not speak too loudly or too softly. It is good for a woman to have a certain amount of pride in her demeanor. Nevertheless, she should know how to make herself desirable and should be gay, playful, and above all, courteous to everyone.

A great deal of advice is given on how to entertain people. All of a lady's guests should be received courteously, but it is important to distinguish the good from the bad. She should not be impolite to anyone, but less desirable guests can be given a less enthusiastic greeting. She should not reveal her troubles or show anger if she is in a bad mood. She should be gay with those who are cheerful and serious with those who are sad, tactfully adjusting herself to the mood of her company. If she is with people who like music, she should sing. Garin advises the lady to welcome troubadours and minstrels (a bit of self-interest here). She should listen to their poems, memorize her favorite passages, and give them gifts so that they will praise her and spread her good fame. By honoring guests as well as she can, she will earn a good reputation.

A number of precepts deal specifically with entertaining men. A lady should not be in an intimate situation with a man unless he is a relative, or she has known him for a long time; otherwise, people will gossip about her. If a man comes to visit her, she should greet him courteously, rising to receive him if she is seated. If he is courteous and honorable, she should invite him to sit beside her. She should listen to his conversation, and if it offends her, it is not necessary to respond with anger. A clever woman has a thousand ways to end a conversation. On the other hand, if his speech pleases her, she should respond with a smile, being careful not to say too much. Garin encourages the lady to flirt with male guests whom she can trust, being careful to be discreet and not to go too far.

Young married women of the aristocracy are given advice on how to play the game of courtly love by Matfre Ermengaud, a friar of Béziers, in the *Breviari d'amor*.[6] This encyclopedic treatise on love is like a compendium of quotes from the troubadours, but its very conventionality makes it valuable as a reflection of the ideas of the time. Ermengaud began the work in 1288. The section addressed to women first discusses dress and deportment. A woman should wear flattering clothes and dress as well as possible according to her rank and income. In private and public, she should always display good manners. She should be cheerful, polite, and skilled in all of the social arts. Ermengaud gives the same advice as Garin lo Brun regarding the reception of guests.

If a man speaks to her of love, she should not get angry, cry out, complain to her husband, or become haughty and proud. If women acted that way, it would be impossible for men to amuse themselves. This comment makes the game aspect of courtly love apparent. Women who are brusque and self-righteous are often less virtuous than those who are sweet and humble. When a deceitful man courts a wise woman, she often perceives his character, and just as he intends to deceive her, she deceives him. She is polite and amiable, promising much and giving nothing, and makes a fool of him. Ermengaud does not entirely approve of this conduct. It is better to speak frankly in order to avoid accusations of falsehood. A woman should be affable and friendly, but she must not do anything dishonorable; she must have the tact to know when to stop so that people will not gossip about her. She should think before she speaks, not speak too loudly or too softly, and not be too familiar with men of another rank. The more attractive a woman is, the more she has to guard her reputation, for it is easy to suspect a pretty woman. She must know how to distinguish the good men from the bad and should not seek the praise of fools. The praise of troubadours, however, will bring her glory.

Ermengaud sets forth a sample dialogue between a lover and a lady who dismisses him because he is not worthy of her. It is better to choose a lover of low rank who is honest than an emperor who is a deceiver. Fidelity is more important than riches, and a lady should not leave a faithful lover for one who is richer. Nevertheless, a woman should not choose a lover of inferior rank or one who is ugly. As a final counsel, Ermengaud advises women to observe the conduct of the good and the bad, and to follow the example of the good. His emphasis on propriety makes it apparent that flirtation among people of the same rank was a perfectly acceptable mode of behavior at the courts of Provence.

Sordello, the thirteenth-century Italian troubadour, addressed his *Ensenhamen d'onor* to both men and women of the aristocracy. The section addressed to women deals with love and deportment.[7] He states that a woman's reputation depends on the man she loves; therefore, she should be sure to choose an honorable lover. If she loves a worthy knight, she cannot lose her good name. Lovers should be loyal to each other, and only death should separate them. Sordello's emphasis on honor and reputation makes it clear that he is discussing platonic love. The abstraction and moral elevation of his discussion anticipates the attitudes of Dante and the Italian *stilnovisti* poets, who deal with love more intellectually than the French troubadours.[8]

Sordello also gives some general advice regarding social conduct. A woman should not speak too much; she should be blind and deaf to unpleasant or vulgar things, conduct herself with moderation and dignity, and have a noble spirit. She should treat guests courteously but not be too familiar with servants. A woman's honor is quickly lost, so she must guard it jealously. In his discussions of love and deportment, Sordello sets forth an elevated ideal that emphasizes honor and courtesy.

In the *Ensenhamen de la donzela*, Amanieu de Sescas addresses specifically a lady-in-waiting in the service of a chatelaine.[9] Amanieu came from Aragon and wrote during the last quarter of the thirteenth century. Like Garin lo Brun, he uses the *reverdie* theme, setting his poem in the month of May. The season makes him think of the lady he loves, who does not love him. While he is lost in thoughts of love, an attractive lady-in-waiting approaches him and asks for advice on how to conduct herself. Naturally, he grants her request.

The poet first describes how the lady-in-waiting should begin her day by preparing her own toilette and that of her mistress. She should get up early to be ready when her mistress calls. She should wash her face, teeth, arms, and hands every morning, cleaning her nails so that they do not have a black border. Her hair should be neatly arranged. Her clothes should be neat and clean without any unsewn seams. Before leaving her room, she should check her appearance in a mirror. She should complete her own toilette before her mistress awakes. If her mistress sleeps in the same room as her husband, she should not enter the room until he has left. She should bring needles and thread in case the clothes of her mistress need to be repaired, a mirror, water, and a towel. She should help her mistress to dress and arrange her hair, not leaving the room until her toilette is completed.

After she has finished helping her mistress to dress, she may join the other people in the hall, where she should politely greet everyone she meets. If someone speaks to her, she should answer courteously. She should walk with grace and dignity, speak in a soft, pleasant voice, and sing melodiously. She should never amuse herself in a vulgar or noisy manner. At the table, she should observe all the rules of etiquette. If she eats with a lady, she should serve her first. If she eats with a man, he should serve her first. She should take a place at the table that is lower than that of her mistress, leaving at least two people between them.

Amanieu offers some good strategies for playing the game of courtly love. If one of the *donzela's* male friends speaks to her of love, she should answer him graciously. If he propositions her, however, she should change the direction of the conversation. She can do this by asking for the news of the day, or better still, she can propose a *demande d'amor*, such as "Which women are prettier, the English or the Gasconnes?" Whatever his response is, she should defend the opposite answer and call upon other people to help decide the question. The *demande d'amor* can thus be used for turning aside another sort of *demande d'amor*. The *donzela* should not choose a lover for his wealth but for his good character and reputation. Lovers should be loyal and faithful to each other. Nothing should occur between them that would damage the honor of a woman. Examples are given of how to respond to statements made by a lover. If someone makes a declaration on the part of another man, a lady should refuse it. With men who seem to be attracted to her but do not dare to say anything, a lady should be amiable and try to amuse them. Amanieu's discussion suggests the popularity of flirtation as a form of social amusement among the aristocracy. A lady-in-waiting had to be adept in the art.

Advice regarding how to play the game of courtly love also appears in the various adaptations of Ovid's *Art of Love*. Some of the works, such as Andreas Capellanus's *Art of Courtly Love*, deal only with love and remain close to Ovid's satirical spirit. Others contain a considerable amount of courtesy book material, which is set forth in a more serious vein. When the translators come to Ovid's discussions of dress, manners, and adornment, they leave their source and describe things in terms of their own age, going into so much detail that these sections are like original courtesy books. Since the works are adaptations of Ovid, we cannot take their recommendations regarding love entirely seriously. What is evident is a playful attitude toward love as a game of flirtation that provides an opportunity for displaying courtly skills.

La Cour d'amour, the earliest work to fall into the *ars amandi*-courtesy book category, was written at the beginning of the thirteenth century in a dialect of southeast Languedoc.[10] It is addressed to married women and young girls of the aristocracy. The author

37

adopts an allegorical framework. Love is portrayed as a princess on Mount Parnassus surrounded by her attendants, who include Fin Amors, Solaz, Ardimen, and Cortesia. Cortesia defines love and gives advice to a lover and his lady. The advice to the lady concerns personal appearance and behavior in the game of love.

The advice regarding appearance is directed at making the woman an appealing sex object. She is told to be scrupulously clean, and to perfume herself and use rose water so that when someone embraces her, her body will smell like a bouquet of flowers. Her eyebrows should be neat and narrow, her teeth small and regular, her lips red and appealing to kiss, and her neck white and smooth. Her hair should be attractively arranged and kept in place by a net, a small crown, or a veil. Her hands should be soft, smooth, and protected by gloves. She should wear a chemise of a fine fabric that is white as the snow in winter, a pretty belt, an attractive purse, and shoes that make her feet appear small. If she wears a hat, it should be placed carefully on her head. A woman should love when she is young, for that is when she is most beautiful; when she is old and has to use false means to appear attractive, she will not be as desirable.

Social skills are important as well as beauty. Praise is acquired through pleasant conversation. One must not be rude or vulgar. A woman should be able to make a man feel intelligent, even if he is a fool. The conversation of love receives the most attention. A woman should know how to respond graciously to her lover. She should never deceive him or lie, or she will lose her credibility. When she is with him, she should be joyful and embrace him, place her arm through his, and let her chest be his pillow. She should tell him she loves him and desires him and swear fidelity to him. When he leaves, she should not reveal he has been with her, and should pretend not to know him in public. Although the *Cour d'amour* treats women mainly as objects of pleasure, it does have a certain refinement.

The *Art d'amor* has a cruder, more Ovidian spirit. It is a free translation of Ovid written by Jacques d'Amiens, a poet of Picardy, toward the middle of the thirteenth century.[11] The first part is addressed to men, the second to married women of the nobility. Like the author of the *Cour d'amour*, Jacques advises women to love while they are young, for that is when they are most appealing. He tells women how to make their appearance pleasing to men. They should dress in good taste and wear colors and fabrics that flatter them: for example, black will make the complexion seem more pale, whereas red will add color to it. A woman should not let her lover see her perform her toilette since it is better for him to think that her beauty is entirely natural. Her hair and her entire body should be clean. Jacques rejects the idea that lack of cleanliness is a sign of godliness and uses the example of the Beguines, religious women who were scrupulously neat and clean, to prove his point. A woman should not have pretty ladies-in-waiting, especially as messengers, since they could become her rivals.

Jacques sets himself up as a master strategist in the game of love. He states that he wishes to teach women to distinguish the true lovers from the false; there are so many deceivers that he does not blame women for being afraid to love. First, he tells women how to get rid of men who do not appeal to them. If a woman is not attracted to a man, she should exhibit her displeasure immediately; if he does not get the message, she should forbid him to speak to her and have her servants show him the door. If he is a man of such high rank that she cannot refuse to receive him, she should avoid being alone with him and reveal her displeasure by the coolness of her manners.

Jacques next tells a woman how to behave with a man who appeals to her. She should not allow him to languish too long, or he might give up his pursuit. She should look at him affectionately, smile at him, show pleasure in his conversation, and jest with him, so that he enjoys her company and perceives her interest in him. If he says something inappropriate, she should ignore it rather than take offense. She should observe his taste and manners and conduct herself to please him.

The author's precepts are directed at making the lady an expert in coquetry. She should allow her lover to embrace her and then pretend she is angry. When she arranges a rendezvous, she should make it difficult and dangerous for him to see her, which will heighten his anticipation. Once he arrives, she should kiss him and embrace him. To see if her lover really cares about her, she should inform him of her plans and see if he turns up where she goes. He will reveal his love most clearly in his generosity. A woman should not ask for gifts, but she may accept them. Since many men are deceivers, a woman might as well accept all she can get so that she will have something when her lover is gone. Jacques adopts Ovid's cynical attitude toward the profit motive. He describes a love that is more sexual and cynical than the kind found in the works of the troubadours.

As in Capellanus's *Art of Courtly Love*, Jacques sets forth several examples of declarations by lovers and responses by ladies. The responses include those of a married woman who wants to remain faithful to her husband, a lady who is afraid of gossip, a lady who fears the falseness and inconstancy of men, an indignant virtuous lady who is insulted by the man's proposition, and a calm wise lady who shows the man the door without too many words or reasons. All the responses are refusals. Even in this frank, Ovidian treatment of love, the end result is merely unsuccessful seduction or flirtation.

La Clef d'amors is another free translation of Ovid, written toward the end of the thirteenth century in a northwest dialect of Normandy.[12] It was probably written by a clerk since the author advises ladies to choose clerks as lovers. It is similar to Jacques d'Amiens's *Art d'amor* in its treatment of love but contains many more details about the dress and manners of the thirteenth century. The author states that a woman should cultivate her beauty to enhance it, and provides detailed directions on how to do this. She should wash her face and body and clean her teeth every day. She should wash her hair frequently, part it evenly, and arrange it in a flattering hairdo. Her eyebrows should be shaped well. Her nails and hands should be well groomed and protected by gloves. When it is hot, she should stay in the shade to avoid sunburn and protect her skin.

She should not simply follow fashion but should wear hairstyles and clothes that are flattering. If she has a pretty neck and shoulders, she should wear décolleté dresses. Her collar and chemise should be neat and clean. Her cloak should have three folds. The author prefers shorter skirts to long, trailing ones. Shoes should be as small as possible to make the feet appear petite. A woman should hide or disguise physical faults. If she is bald or has thin hair, she should wear wigs or hairpieces. If she is grey, she should tint her hair. She should use makeup but not let her lover see her apply it. If she is too short, it is better for her to be seen when seated. If she is too thin, she should wear many garments and heavy fabrics. If she has ugly feet, she should not be seen barefoot. If her breasts are too large, she should tie bands around them. If her hands are ugly, she should not make gestures with them. If her breath is bad, she should not be too close to people when speaking. If her teeth are ugly, she should not open her mouth too wide.

A woman should not laugh too loudly or too long. Some women know how to cry on command and use this ability to their advantage. A woman should walk slowly and gracefully, sing with a melodious voice, play musical instruments, dance, read romances, play social games, and be a good conversationalist. If she loses at gambling, she should not become angry or swear. She should have good manners at the dinner table as well as the gaming table.

The advice regarding love follows the other works. Once again, women are advised to love when young. Marriage is attacked as a prison for women. To be worthy of love, a woman should be pleasant, wise, courteous, sincere, gentle, humble, and honest. A woman may attract lovers at church, dances, carols, weddings, public celebrations, and on pilgrimages. Her beauty is wasted if it remains hidden. She should not trust flatterers or stingy lovers. When someone sends her a message of love, she should accept it but delay in answering and give an ambiguous response. To avoid being discovered, she should use only one messenger, write so that the message is hard to read, and use secret codes. Discretion and prudence are needed in love affairs. When with her lover, she should be gay and playful and make him believe she loves him above everything else. Clerks are recommended as the best lovers. (Here, we may have a clerk-poet flirting with his female patron.)

Aristocratic women, who were the model for the courtly lady, gained a certain amount of prestige and influence from the game of courtly love. After centuries of institutionalized misogyny within the Church, an alternative image which exalted woman could only do her good. Courtly love made the honoring of woman and a profeminist stance part of the aristocratic chivalric code. A knight who played the role of a courtly lover declared himself a servant and took a lady as his master. To indicate his attitude of homage, he addressed her as *midons* (derived from *mi*, my, and *dominus*, lord).[13] Nevertheless, no real power was involved. The homage of the knight to his lady was only a word game. The so-called courts of love were merely literary gatherings where people read poems or romances, debated *demandes d'amor*, and played word games of flirtation. Women exerted a significant literary and social influence, however, as patrons and members of the audience.

At the courts of Provence, women were not only patrons but also poets.[14] The position of the women troubadours, or *trobairitz* as they were called in Provençal, was different from that of the male troubadours. The male troubadours were often professional poets seeking patronage, whereas the *trobairitz* were aristocratic women writing for personal rather than professional reasons.[15] This allowed them to use their poems as vehicles of self-expression. Sometimes they adopted the same poses as the men, such as that of the humble lover; but more often they broke out of the conventional roles to speak in clear, natural voices. Their language is direct, unambiguous, and personal, with an intimate tone that is usually lacking in works by the male troubadours. There is less striving for cleverness and sophistication, more concentration on emotion and experience.

The *trobairitz* write of love, but they often abandon the conventional courtly formulas. They do not play the formal, distant *midons*, nor do they place their lovers in that role. They express anger, frustration, impatience, resentment, eagerness, humor, and sexual passion. For example, in the following lines, Tibors is the reverse of the distant *midons*.

> Sweet handsome friend, I can tell you truly
> that I've never been without desire
> since it pleased you that I have you as my courtly lover;
> nor did a time ever arrive, sweet handsome friend,
> when I didn't want to see you often;
> nor did I ever feel regret,
> nor did it ever come to pass, if you went off angry,
> that I felt joy until you had come back.[16]

The Countess of Dia unambiguously expresses physical desire.

> How I wish just once I could caress
> that chevalier with my bare arms,
> for he would be in ecstasy
> if I'd just let him lean his head against my breast.[17]

Isabella angrily rebukes Elias Cairel.

42

Elias Cairel, you're a phoney
if I ever saw one,
like a man who says he's sick
when he hasn't got the slightest pain.
If you'd listen, I'd give you good advice:
go back to your cloister,
and don't dare pronounce my name again
except in prayer to the patriarch Ivan.[18]

In these poems, we get beyond the artificial conventions of courtly love and hear real women addressing real men. The game of courtly love thus created conditions at the courts of Provence that allowed women to become poets who spoke in their own voices and broke out of conventional poses.

The ideas of courtly love were introduced into the North by Eleanor of Aquitaine, first in her marriage to Prince Louis of France and later in her marriage to Henry II of England.[19] She established a court at Westminster that became a center of literary culture. The poems and romances she patronized drew their material from the legends of Rome, Byzantium, and Camelot; the lyrics drew their inspiration from the courtly love tradition of the troubadours.[20] Thomas of Britain wrote his *Tristram and Ysolt* under her inspiration, Wace dedicated his *Roman de Brut* to her, and Marie de France composed her *Lais* at her court.

The Countess Marie, daughter of Eleanor and Louis VII, turned the court of Champagne into an important literary center.[21] It was once assumed that Marie was influenced by Eleanor, but this has been called into question. Marie was only seven years old when Eleanor left the court of France, and there is no documentary evidence that they communicated after that time.[22] Nevertheless, lack of documentation does not mean that meetings did not occur. The probability of a relationship between Marie and her mother seems strong in view of connections between Marie and Eleanor's sons and daughters-in-law, circumstances that placed them in close proximity on several occasions, and the fact that they were mother and daughter.[23]

What is certain is that Marie was one of the outstanding literary patrons of her day. Her tastes were not exclusively courtly since a French verse translation of Genesis and paraphrase of one of the psalms were among the works composed for her. Courtly works written for her included a lyric by Gace Brulé, *Eracle* by Gautier d'Arras, and *The Knight of the Cart* by Chrétien de Troyes.[24] Chrétien states that Marie provided him with the *matière* (subject matter) and the *sens* (manner of treatment) of the romance.[25] This poem, which glorifies Lancelot's adulterous love for Guenevere and his humble service to her, is a comic treatment of a courtly love relationship. Courtly love is illustrated by dialogues and elaborately codified in *The Art of Courtly Love* by Andreas Capellanus, a chaplain at Marie's court. Andreas identifies women who presided over courts of love, including Eleanor of Aquitaine, Marie of Champagne, Adele of Champagne, Ermengarde of Narbonne, and Isabelle of Flanders.[26] These "courts" were probably literary salons. Most of the women he mentions were important literary patrons who supported the avant-garde literature of their day.

Women supported the literature of courtly love because it was ostensibly feminist. Nevertheless, although courtly love exalted women and placed them on a pedestal, it also turned them into objects of pleasure and easily could be used to exploit them. Christine de Pizan was well aware of this aspect of the game of love and saw it mainly as a tool of seduction. Therefore, she was one of its critics rather than a supporter. Her most thorough critique occurs in the *Livre des trois vertus* (also known as the *Trésor de la Cité des dames*), a mirror for princesses and women of other social classes written about 1405. Christine favored romantic married love but totally rejected "folle amour," the name she gives to extramarital involvements. She provides detailed instructions for a governess to enable her to prevent a young princess from having an affair.[27] If any man tries to approach her mistress to speak of love, the governess should first gain his confidence and then tell him that her lady is entirely devoted to her husband, and she herself will do all she can to encourage her to remain faithful. If the governess serves a lady who seems to want to have an affair, she should try first to dissuade her. If this does not work, she should quickly leave her service so as not to be blamed but should write to her to try to change her mind. Christine provides a sample letter, adopted from her earlier *Duc des vrais amants*, in which she warns against illicit love and shows how it can impair a woman's character, reputation, and position. She believed that women should occupy themselves with more serious concerns rather than with the false flattery and potential danger of flirtation.

Christine's perceptive criticism alerts us to the fact that the game of courtly love was a mixed blessing for women. After centuries of clerical antifeminism, an alternative ideal that was ostensibly feminist was a welcome change, especially since it was supported by the aristocracy. The code of courtly love provided a useful function for the aristocracy, acting as a safety valve in a society of frustrated bachelors and chaste wives whose marriages were arranged for political reasons. Social acceptance of the game of flirtation may have reduced the actual occurrence of adultery. The game of courtly love allowed women some freedom in their relations with men and helped develop their influence as literary patrons. In Provence, they even became poets. Yet all of this apparent exaltation of women gave them little real power. The right to flirt is not a very significant freedom. In the courtesy books influenced by the ideal of courtly love, women are at best a passive source of inspiration for men and at worst a sex object for their pleasure. In many cases, the chivalric placement of women on a pedestal was a compensation for and a romanticization of their lack of power.

IV

Woman as Wife and Mother

At the very time that courtly eroticism was flourishing, a powerful current of a different kind also was developing: the exaltation of marriage, the praise of the fruitful couple entrusted with the husbanding of a patrimony by the deliberate choice of two families and engaged in legitimate procreation.[1] This ideal also pervaded the literature of entertainment. If Chrétien de Troyes wrote the *Knight of the Cart* in which he celebrated courtly love, he also wrote *Erec and Enide* in which he celebrated marriage with much more enthusiasm. A number of romances glorify the founding of a family, including *Melusine*, which tells the story of the fairy Melusine, a supposed progenitor of the house of Lusignan, and *Ponthus and Sidoine*, which deals with the fortunes of the Tour-Landry family.

In *Medieval Marriage*, Georges Duby identifies marriage as the central institution of medieval society.[2] By uniting two individuals born of two different houses to ensure the survival of one of those houses, marriage bestowed official recognition and singled out those unions that society legitimized as a means of perpetuating itself. This is why marriage was supposed to be a public, ceremonial act. It called for a celebration that assembled large numbers of people to attend a central rite. Marriage was founded on an agreement between two houses in which one of the houses gave up a woman and the other one received her. The exchange involved her anticipated motherhood, her "blood" and all that it brought to the new family in terms of ancestry and claims to inheritances.

For most women, marriage was the only available career. The only choices open to aristocratic women were to marry or enter a

46

convent. A father or a rich male relative provided an upper-class girl with either a dowry to buy her a husband or a contribution to gain her entrance into a convent. It is not surprising that many women entered convents without having any vocation for the career of a nun. The middle-class girl either married or was apprenticed to a trade, but she was in a much better position as the wife or widow of a tradesman.

A medieval wife played an important economic role. As head of her household, she was practically a business manager. If she was a noblewoman, she had to supervise a large staff of ladies-in-waiting, pages, and servants. Wealthy members of the landed gentry and the middle class imitated the aristocracy in maintaining a large household since having a large number of servants was a status symbol and an indication of power. Less prosperous wives of merchants and artisans had to get along with fewer servants and do many jobs themselves. The wives of poor artisans and peasants had to do all of the household tasks themselves. These tasks were considerable, for many items were produced in the home during the Middle Ages. The castle or manor was practically a self-sufficient economic unit, at least in regard to daily staples. Even in the modest cottage, many items were produced for home consumption and sometimes for sale.

Since the role of a wife was most important for a medieval woman, it is not surprising that the largest number of courtesy books are addressed to the married woman or the woman who intends to marry. The books fall into several different genres. Some of them are personal books of instruction addressed by fathers, husbands, or mothers to daughters. Occasionally, the author is known. In most cases, the works are anonymous, and some of them are so general that the parental stance might be fictional. Other works are general treatises of instruction addressed to married women. Still others are more comprehensive treatments of women's role in society, including sections addressed to wives. Since there are some significant differences between the works written by men and those written ostensibly by women, I will divide the treatises into those two categories.

Although the social ideal is similar in all of the works, individual authors reveal themselves somewhat in their emphasis on particular aspects of life and in their attitudes toward women, whether it is the particular women they are addressing or women in general.

For instance, Saint Louis reveals his spirituality and lack of worldliness in the two letters of instruction he wrote for his daughters. The *Enseignements à sa fille Isabelle* were written for Isabelle after she had married Thibaut, King of Navarre, in 1255.[3] Although the work was written by a king for a queen, it concerns only Isabelle's duties as a Christian, as a wife, and as a daughter and contains nothing about her role as a ruler. Most of the precepts concern attitudes and behavior within the religious sphere.

Louis states that he is writing the work for his daughter with his own hand since she is more likely to listen to him than to other people because of the love she has for him.[4] First of all, he exhorts her to love God with all her heart and all her power. She should do things that would please God and avoid things that would displease Him. She should prefer to die rather than commit a mortal sin, confess often, take pleasure in going to church, and listen attentively to sermons. If she experiences any affliction, she should suffer it in patience and believe that it is deserved. If she experiences any good fortune, she should not become proud. She should have pity for unfortunate people and give alms to the poor. Rather than spending a great deal of money on clothing or jewels, she should dress modestly and use a good part of her income for alms. She should be obedient and humble to her father, mother, and husband. The women in her service should be moral and pious. The best way to enforce discipline among them is by setting a good example herself. Louis closes the treatise by wishing his daughter well and asking her to have prayers and masses said for him after his death.

Similar material appears in the *Enseignements* written for one of Louis's other daughters. It is addressed to a married woman and was meant either for Blanche, who married Ferdinand, Prince of Castille, or for Marguerite, who married Jean, Duke of Brabant. The focus is on religion, as in the *Enseignements* addressed to Isabelle, but there is more advice regarding social conduct. Louis tells his daughter to avoid the sins of pride, lechery, laziness, and gluttony. Instead of giving her an elaborate set of table manners, he tells her to think of God while at the table.

> Daughter, when you come to the table to eat, you must not seek only pleasure for your mouth but also nourish-

ment, and think of God so that you do not take more than
you need.[5]

Louis offers several precepts in this letter regarding propriety of
speech. He tells his daughter to think before speaking so that she
will not say anything she will regret, to speak with reason, and to
utter few words. When speaking to a man, she should not say
anything that could be interpreted as a flirtatious remark.

> Daughter, if you want to speak to a man, make sure that
> you do not say anything that might seem improper; but
> speak words that are edifying, by which one can judge
> that you are a wise young lady and well instructed.[6]

He warns his daughter not to be familiar with any man who is not
moral and religious. She should not be too familiar with anyone,
although she should be humble and generous. This letter is just as
idealistic as the one addressed to Isabelle, but there is more guidance regarding behavior in the secular world.

The point of view of a member of the landed gentry is expressed in the *Livre du chevalier de la Tour-Landry*, written between
1371 and 1372 by Geoffrey de la Tour-Landry, a knight of Poitou,
for his three daughters. The book enjoyed considerable popularity
during the Middle Ages. It was copied many times and had become
widely known by the end of the fifteenth century. There are still at
least twenty-one manuscripts of the French text in existence. An
English translation, extant in one imperfect manuscript, was made
during the reign of Henry VI. Caxton made a new English translation entitled *The Book of the Knight of the Tower*, which he printed
in 1484. A German version entitled *Der Ritter vom Turn* was made
by Marquart von Stein, ostensibly for his own two daughters, and
published at Basle in 1493.[7]

The Book of the Knight of the Tower is written entirely from a
man's point of view. The Knight wanted to turn women into docile
creatures who would cause men the least possible trouble and expense. He places a great deal of emphasis on religious activities.
This emphasis comes not from his own faith, but from his desire to
keep women secluded and to make them the custodians of morality.
According to the Knight, the worse a husband is, the more his wife

should pray for his salvation. He states that women should frequently pray and go to church. Within the church, they should behave modestly and should pay attention to the service. They should choose an honest confessor and confess frequently. He highly recommends the practice of fasting.

His approval of fasting is tied to his frugality. He tells women to eat simply and to drink very little. They should not waste food or give the best pieces of food to pets, should dress simply and modestly, and should not spend too much money on clothes. The Knight is particularly disturbed by women's desire to wear new fashions. Many of his anecdotes concern women who came to bad ends or lost suitors because they indulged in foreign, overly elaborate, or impractical fashions. From the Knight's point of view, one of the worst things that can happen to a girl is to lose the opportunity for a good marriage. He was obviously worried about having to marry off three daughters.

The Knight considers the virtues of chastity, humility, obedience, and modesty the most important feminine qualities. Women should have a modest demeanor. They should not wear makeup, pluck their eyebrows, or tint their hair. The Knight regards feminine beauty as an expensive liability rather than an asset. A young girl should not be vain or flirtatious. Although flirtatious behavior may amuse men, it will not attract them as husbands. He tells an anecdote about rejecting a girl his family had chosen as a wife for him because she was too flirtatious.

The Knight believes that women should remain at home and should not always want to go to jousts, dances, and banquets. If they must go to a banquet, they should be suitably accompanied, preferably by a relative, and should behave modestly. A woman should be modest in her speech, should not talk too much, not contradict her husband, not jest (particularly with men), and not curse.

According to the Knight, a married woman should maintain an ideal standard of behavior regardless of the actions of her husband. She should be absolutely faithful and not speak with other men of love. She should not be jealous, even if her husband gives her cause. The Knight frankly maintains a double sexual standard. He sees infidelity as a mortal sin for a woman but scarcely a venial sin for a man.

The Knight also has a double standard regarding the expression of anger. He states that a woman should not show anger or answer back her husband. If he becomes angry, she should endure his tirades with patience. She should display complete obedience, especially in front of others. He tells a story of a burgher's wife whose husband broke her nose because of disobedience.

> After this a woman in no maner wyse ought stryue ageynst her husbond, ne answere hym so that he take therby displaysyre, lyke as dyde the wyf of a burgeys whiche answerd to her husband so noiously and shamefully to fore the peple, that he bicam angry and felle to see hym self so rewlyd to fore the peple, that he had therof shame. And he said to her and bad her ones or twyes that she shold be stylle and leue, but she wold not & her husbond whiche was wrothe smote her with his fyste to the erthe. And smote her with his foote on the vysage so that he brake her nose, by whiche she was euer after al disfygured. And soo by her ryotte and ennoye she gate her a croked nose, moche euyll. It had ben moche better for her that she had holden her stylle and hadde suffred, yet it is reson and ryght that the husbonde haue the hyhe wordes, and it is but honoure to a good woman to suffre and holde her in pees, and leue the haultayn langage to her husbond and lord. And also it is in the contrarye to a woman grete shame and vylonye to stryue ageynst her husbond be it wrong or right.[8]

The Knight matter-of-factly relates several other examples of wife-beating.[9] In telling the stories, he criticizes the disobedience of the wives without saying anything about the brutality of the husbands. At one point he associates wife beating with the middle class and states that gentlewomen should not be handled that way.[10] Nevertheless, he acknowledges that disobedient gentlewomen risk being beaten and apparently considers a woman's disobedience a much worse fault than wife-beating.

According to one major principle of the Knight, a wife should compensate for her husband's faults. He states that a woman should not gossip behind her husband's back and not reveal his secrets. She should defend him and support him even if he is bad. The worse a husband is, the better a wife should be to make up for him.

> And therfor it is good and necessary to an euyl man to haue a good wyf and of holy lyf. And the more that the good wyf knoweth her husbond more felon and cruel, and grete synnar, the more she ought to make gretter abstynences and good dedes for the loue of god. And yf the one suffre not the other, that is to vnderstonde, yf the good dyd suffre & supported not the euylle, all shold go to perdicion. [11]

Although the Knight claims that the good should suffer the evil, he says nothing about good husbands putting up with bad wives. He maintains a double standard regarding sexuality, self-restraint, and overall morality. For a "successful" marriage he proposes that women should be models of morality and patience whose virtues compensate for the faults of men.

A more balanced attitude is found in the *Castigos y dotrinas que un sabio dava a sus hijas*. It was written in the fifteenth century by a Spanish father who belonged to the middle class and was possibly a merchant. [12] He believes that all women wish to marry and sets forth advice regarding the duties of a wife to help his daughters achieve a good marriage. Virtue is more desirable and more important in a wife than riches, lineage, or beauty. A woman should be obedient and humble to her husband. He cites the story of Griselda as an example, stating that if a poor man's daughter could be so obedient, a girl of good family should be even better.

The author states that chastity is the most important virtue in a woman, citing Saint Augustine and Saint Ambrose as his authorities. He warns his daughters that a husband can kill his wife for unchaste behavior, and all the goods of the family become his. This, in fact, was a law set forth in the *Siete Partidas*. [13] A woman should be chaste in appearance as well as in behavior. Modest dress is even more important when her husband is absent. It is an offense to God, the Creator, when a woman uses makeup or tints her hair, and women who do so will be punished in hell. If a woman uses makeup, her husband and other people will suspect her of immodesty. Moreover, it is bad for her health.

The author advises his daughters not to go out of the house frequently. His ideas regarding seclusion are stricter than those of most authors and probably reflect the Arab influence prevalent in Spain. He states that a woman who goes out often shows little prudence. A woman should not attend games, jousts, or bull fights. It is even more important to stay at home when her husband is absent.

A woman should be modest in her gestures and speech. She should not listen to discussions or jests that are inappropriate for her ears, flattery, or propositions from men. To avoid suspicion, she should neither receive a man in her home when her husband is absent nor speak with men at the doors or windows of her house. In the absence of her husband, she should have a maid sleep in her room. A woman should be moderate in eating and drinking and not drink wine, which leads to lechery, imprudent speech, and immodesty.

A woman should maintain peace in her family and household. She should treat her neighbors and relatives well, keep her husband from making enemies, and not be jealous of her husband. A jealous wife is always unhappy, does not take proper care of her household, and makes life difficult for her husband. If her husband is unfaithful, she can threaten to refuse to maintain his household. If that has no effect, she can discuss the problem with a trusted relative. The author has a more just attitude than the Knight of the Tower and does not expect a woman simply to put up with infidelity.

A good wife should be prudent and thrifty in managing her household. Since a woman does not earn money, at least she should not waste it. She should neither live beyond her income nor have too many servants. She should be fair to servants and treat them well, which will make them work more industriously. She should not spend much money when her husband is away but should eat simply and refrain from amusements. The author ends by citing Solomon's description of the good woman of Proverbs as an example of the perfect wife.[14]

The *Ménagier de Paris* was written by a husband rather than a father, but since he was old enough to be his wife's grandfather, it has a paternal tone. The author was a wealthy bourgeois official in the service of the government of Charles V.[15] Since his name is not known, he is referred to as the Ménagier (household manager) of Paris. He was probably close to sixty when he wrote the work and had married an orphan of fifteen from a family of higher social rank. In the first week of their marriage, she asked him to be indulgent of her youth and to instruct her privately in her duties so that she would not be embarrassed in front of guests or servants; to comply with her request, he wrote this treatise. Because the Ménagier's wife was so young, she was under the supervision of a duenna, Dame Agnes the Beguine, but he anticipated her assuming more freedom and responsibility.

The first part of the treatise is divided into nine articles and deals with religious and moral instruction. We find the usual ideal of docility, modesty, and obedience. The first article concerns religious matters. The Ménagier sets forth prayers that his wife should say in the morning and evening. They are identified by their first lines in Latin but translated into French, which suggests that his wife did not know Latin.

Speaking of activities appropriate for the morning brings the Ménagier to the subject of dress. He recognizes that dress is an important means of demonstrating one's rank. Dignity, suitability, and neatness are of the utmost importance. A woman should not indulge in new fashions. She should not use too much or too little adornment. Rich fabrics and furs were a means of displaying one's wealth, and the Ménagier did not object to such garments for himself or his wife. In fact, he gives elaborate instructions for their care. He did object to a bold, careless appearance.

The second article deals with suitable behavior in church and town. The Ménagier's discussion reveals that he expects women to walk alone or in groups in the street. He stresses the importance of having a modest demeanor, being suitably accompanied (he is particularly concerned about this because of his wife's youth), and associating only with respectable people. He allows his wife some of the pleasures of youth, such as weaving garlands, singing, and attending dances as long as they are given by people in their own social circle.

The third article begins with more religious instruction, including a discourse on the Mass and one on confession. The topic of confession leads to a discussion of the seven deadly sins and the virtues that combat them: pride, which is opposed by humility; envy by kindness; anger by gentleness, sloth by diligence; avarice by generosity; gluttony by temperance; and lechery by chastity. The Ménagier tells his wife that she will be able to learn more on these topics by listening to the sermons she will hear in their parish and elsewhere. He also approves of her reading moral and religious treatises and offers to place at her disposal French versions of the Bible, the *Golden Legend*, the *Apocalypse*, and the *Life of the Fathers* by Saint Jerome, all of which he owns. He mentions that he has other books in French as well; so he apparently owned a good library.

In the fourth article on chastity, the Ménagier tactfully assures his wife that he does not doubt her but is discussing the subject so that she will have the information to instruct their daughters or friends. He states that the woman who lives continently, giving herself only to her husband, can be considered a virgin. This was a way of adapting the doctrines of the Church Fathers for married women. Unlike the Church Fathers and most men who wrote instructions for their wives, he approves of his wife marrying a second time after he is dead. In fact, one of his avowed reasons for writing the treatise is to make his wife a more accomplished woman for her second husband. To illustrate the virtue of chastity, he uses the examples of Susanna and Lucrece and discusses the customs followed by the queens of France: to prevent suspicion they embrace no man except the king and read sealed letters in private only if they are from the king. Similarly, the Ménagier advises his wife to read private letters only from her husband and to write only to him. If she receives letters from other men, she should have them read publicly. If she should have to write to another man, she should use the services of a scribe.

The fifth article concerns love and relations with men. He exhorts his wife to love her husband and be devoted to him, using the examples of Sarah, Rebecca, and Rachel. She should be intimate with her husband and moderately familiar with relatives but should not be familiar with any other men. She should be sure to avoid lazy young men who spend money too freely, men of the court, and men who have a reputation for leading a free life.

The sixth and longest article in the first section reflects the importance placed upon obedience as a wifely virtue. The Ménagier cites Ephesians V:22-24 on the duty of wives to obey their husbands, the husband being "head" of the wife, as Christ is head of the Church.[16] He states that a woman should obey all the commands of her husband in large matters and in small. She should always do what she knows will please him. If she knows he would forbid something, she should not do it and not try to circumvent his disapproval by not asking him. She should not contradict him or answer him back, particularly in front of others. He uses several examples to illustrate the virtue of obedience, including the story of Griselda. Nevertheless, he does not demand a Griselda-like obedience from his wife and tells her, "je ne suis mie marquis, et ne vous ay prise bergière" [I am not a marquis and have not taken you as a shepherdess.][17] His attitude is reasonable and compromising, and he sees himself and his wife as partners in the running of the household. Nevertheless, he affirms that obedience is the best way to acquire a husband's love.

Article seven is a practical section dealing with the care of one's husband. The Ménagier describes the discomforts a man faces in going about his business in all kinds of weather in the country and the city. He will gladly return home if his wife provides physical comforts and greets him cheerfully.

> Wherefore love your husband's person carefully, and I pray you keep him in clean linen, for that is your business, and because the trouble and care of outside affairs lieth with men, so must husbands take heed, and go and come, and journey hither and thither, in rain and wind, in snow and hail, now drenched, now dry, now sweating, now shivering, ill-fed, ill-lodged, ill-warmed and ill-bedded. And naught harmeth him, because he is upheld by the hope that he hath of the care which his wife will take of him on his return, and of the ease, the joys and the pleasures which she will do him, or cause to be done to him in her presence; to be unshod before a good fire, to have his feet washed and fresh shoes and hose, to be given good food and drink, to be well served and well looked after, well bedded in white sheets and nightcaps, well covered with good furs, and assuaged with other joys and desports, privities, loves and secrets whereof I am silent. And the next day fresh shirts and garments. Certes, fair sister, such services make a man love and desire to return to his home and to see his goodwife, and to be distant with others.[18]

The Ménagier's description provides a vivid picture of the weary merchant or businessman returning to his fireside after a hard day and enjoying the comforts of his home. By taking care of her husband herself instead of leaving the task to servants, a wife demonstrates her love for him.

The eighth article concerns the language appropriate for a woman. The Ménagier advises his wife not to speak too much, not to say anything in jest or mockery that she might regret, not to laugh too much, and to speak humbly and courteously to everyone. It is inappropriate for a woman to show anger, particularly to her husband. She should not gossip with other women and not reveal the secrets of her husband. A wife and husband should uphold each other's honor. The Ménagier relates several anecdotes from ancient history and contemporary life to show how couples have done this, even going so far as to accept illegitimate offspring. His anecdotes concern husbands who forgive and cover up for wives as well as wives who protect husbands. In the ninth article, he shows how a woman can advise her husband against acting foolishly, using the tale of Melibee as an exemplum.

The second part of the treatise concerns the care of the household and is a rich mine of information regarding life in a bourgeois Parisian household of the fourteenth century. It begins on a theoretical level with a transcript of *Le Chemin de povreté et de richesse* by Jehan Bruyant, a notary of the king at the Chatelet of Paris. In this allegorical dream vision, the author shows how diligence and virtuous behavior lead to prosperity. Following the transcript is the practical information provided by the Ménagier. He lists the kinds of plants that could be cultivated in a town garden and gives the proper times of year for planting, grafting, and other gardening procedures. He discusses the kinds of workers whose services filled the needs of a medieval household in town and on a country estate. He did not expect his wife to hire them since she was so young, but an older woman would have had this responsibility. Some workers were hired to perform a particular job or to do seasonal work: porters and wheelbarrow men to carry burdens; coopers to make and repair barrels and casks; packers, reapers, mowers, threshers, grape pickers, basket bearers, and wine pressers. Other workers were hired for a special craft or to do piecework, such as dressmakers, furriers, bakers, butchers, and shoemakers. Still others were hired as domestic servants and became part of the household. In hiring domestic servants, the Ménagier recommends checking references carefully. Only reliable workers should be hired, and they should be paid well so that they will stay on the job. Accurate records should be kept regarding payments to workers and all other household expenses.

The Ménagier discusses the daily chores that have to be done in town and in the country, revealing that he himself owned a country estate. In town, the chambermaids have to sweep out and clean the entrances to the house and the hall, dust and shake out the covers and cushions which are on the benches, and clean and straighten out the other rooms in the house. Household pets have to be taken care of. In the country, the workers who look after the farm animals, such as the shepherd, the oxherd, and the dairymaid, have to be supervised.

The Ménagier was apparently a gourmet and wanted his wife to be able to supervise the purchasing and preparation of food. He provides a list of the butchers in Paris and the approximate number of sheep, oxen, pigs, and calves each of them slaughtered. He describes how poultry should be slaughtered and tells his wife how to choose fresh game and fish. To help his wife plan dinners and suppers for company, he includes a number of suggested menus. These are followed by a recipe book, which is adapted from the *Livre fort excellent de cuisine* by Taillevent, the chef of Charles V.[19] The recipes reveal the medieval predilection for elaborate dishes and spicy food. Among them are recipes for hares in civey, a spicy sauce made of onions, bread, vinegar, ginger, pepper, nutmeg, and cinnamon; soringue of eels, a purée made of skinned eels, toasted bread, onions, parsley, ginger, cinnamon, cloves, saffron, vinegar, and wine; and hippocras, wine spiced with cinnamon, cloves, ginger, nutmeg, and galingale. Medieval recipe books included medicinal recipes as well as ones for food. The Ménagier includes remedies for toothache and the bite of a dog.

The Ménagier completed only the first section of the third part of his work, which is a treatise on hunting with the hawk. Hunting with the hawk was less expensive than other forms of the chase and was popular among wealthy members of the bourgeoisie. This variety of hunting was the only form considered suitable for ladies. A large group of men and women usually engaged in it together. In addition to this section on hunting, the Ménagier had planned a section on such parlor games as word games, dice, chess, and cards, as well as one on divining and astrology, which were popular pastimes. He wanted his wife to be skilled in all of the activities of people of their social class, the amusements as well as the tasks. The Ménagier shows himself to be a kind, generous husband who respects his wife, wants her to enjoy herself and develop her abilities, and considers her a full partner in the running of their elaborate household. Of course, we are dealing with individual authors rather than class representatives; but one cannot help comparing the Ménagier's attitudes with those of the Knight of the Tower and seeing that a member of the bourgeoisie could be much more "chivalric" toward women than a knight.

We now turn to more general works written by male authors. The *Chastoiement des dames*, composed by Robert of Blois during the third quarter of the thirteenth century, is a treatise of instruction addressed to women of the aristocracy. Although Robert was a clerk, he emphasizes social behavior rather than religious and moral obligations. He advises women to be temperate in all things, including eating, drinking, and personal adornment, but does not insist on a self-denying asceticism. A woman should be courteous to everybody and know how to greet, serve, and entertain people. She should not talk too much or too little. If she talks too much, people will think she is domineering, whereas if she talks too little, people will think she is proud. She should not show anger and not quarrel with others. All of these precepts illustrate woman's role as the server, harmonizer, and peacemaker in social relationships.

Robert offers many precepts concerning deportment and appearance. A woman should walk with grace and dignity, moving slowly, taking small steps, and keeping her gaze directly forward. Her clothes should be clean, neat, and modest; low necklines and skirts that expose the legs should be avoided. A woman who exposes her body will earn a bad reputation. The only parts of the body that should be exposed are the face, throat, and hands. Robert does not object to feminine beauty as long as it is displayed modestly. He even provides hints for improving pale color (drinking wine is one of his suggestions) and doing away with bad breath.

Robert provides detailed advice regarding table manners. A woman should not eat or drink too much. Drunkenness is particularly objectionable in a woman. She should not talk or laugh while eating or put pieces of food into her mouth that are too hot, too cold, or too big. As a gesture of courtesy, she should not take the best pieces of food for herself but leave them for others. When drinking, she should wipe her mouth so as not to get grease on the cup. She should not get her hands greasy. All of these rules create an impression of delicacy and deference to others.

Robert describes the behavior that is suitable in church. A woman should behave with dignity since many people will observe her. She should not laugh or talk but kneel and say her prayers, keeping her mind on the service. Robert's emphasis is social rather than spiritual; he is concerned with the impression a woman will make on her neighbors.

Robert advises a woman how to behave with her husband and other men. She should be courteous but not bold. If she looks at a man too frequently, she may lead him to believe she is attracted to him: "Li regart sont d'amor mesaige" [looks are the messengers of love].[20] As for allowing her breast to be touched,

> Make sure that no man places his hand on your breast,
> Except he who has the right to do it.
> You should know that brooches were first invented for
> this purpose,
> That no man would place his hand on the breast of a
> woman if he did not have the right, if she were not mar-
> ried to him.
> The husband can do this without penalty
> And can take the rest at pleasure.
> When your husband wishes to embrace you,
> Suffer his advances obediently,
> As the monk obeys his abbot.[21]

In discussing a woman's response to her husband's sexual advances, Robert uses a metaphor of obedience (the monk obeying his abbot) rather than one of enjoyment. A married woman was supposed to demonstrate her chastity by not enjoying sex too much.

Robert advises a woman to reject any kind of sexual advance made to her by a man other than her husband. A woman should not let any man except her husband kiss her, because if a man and woman enjoy kissing each other, they will want to go further. If a

60

man speaks to a woman of love, she should turn him down, stating that she is faithful to her husband. Robert provides a sample dialogue, using the kind of "lines" found in Andreas Capellanus's *De arte honeste amandi* and other medieval *ars amandi*. Robert states that if the man is really interested in the woman, he will not be discouraged by the refusal but will come back for more. Robert's acceptance of flirtation in his portrait of the chaste, modest wife shows how much the ideal of courtly love had been domesticated.

The *Reggimento e costumi di donna* is a more comprehensive treatise dealing with the roles of women in medieval society and the manners the author considered suitable for them. It was composed between 1307 and 1315 by Francesco Barberino, a doctor of law in Florence.[22] He addressed women of all social classes, from princesses to serfs, and in all cases deemed their relationships with men most important. He classifies women as young girls before marriage, girls at an age suitable for marriage, girls who have lost the hope for marriage, wives, widows, and widows who remarry.

Barberino provides a great deal of advice for the married woman, beginning with the day of her wedding.[23] Before the wedding, the bride should be instructed by her mother regarding her sexual duties. The bride should be timid and reserved throughout the wedding ceremony and the celebration. She should not reach for the ring or answer yes too readily. The main virtues of a wife are obedience, constancy, and chastity. She should be faithful to her husband even if he is unfaithful to her. Once again, we have a double sexual standard. A woman should be pious and charitable, should have an honest confessor, and should go to confession frequently. She should hire honorable servants and maintain an orderly, proper atmosphere in her household. She should guard her own reputation and be open to honest criticism. If her husband becomes angry or beats her, she should remain submissive and humble and endure his anger with patience. She should try to have a pacifying influence on her husband's behavior with her and others. She should be a thrifty housewife, taking care of her husband's clothing, furniture, and provisions. She should help her husband to dress, consulting with his tailors to select clothes that suit him. When her husband is sick, she should pamper him and nurse him back to good health. On the other hand, when she is sick, she should hide her discomfort and pain, except from the doctor. Barberino advises a wife to be an ideal nurse and servant but gives little consideration to her feelings and needs.

The works written ostensibly by women contain the same social ideal as those by men, but they show more sympathy for the feelings and interests of women. In dealing with the anonymous works, we do not know whether they were composed by women or by men playing the roles of women. It is possible that male writers assumed a female narrative persona to make their books more marketable to the growing audience of middle-class women, who were gaining substantial legal rights and social mobility.

The question of male or female authorship is a key problem concerning *Die Winsbekin*, a poem in Middle High German written in the thirteenth century. It survives in the same manuscript as *Der Winsbeke*, a book of advice from a Bavarian knight to his son, but is written in a different hand.[24] Scholars continue to debate whether or not both poems are by the same author.[25]

The poem assumes the form of a dialogue between a mother, a Bavarian lady who has been at court, and her daughter. The mother begins by exhorting her daughter to love and praise God.[26] She states that she wishes to teach her to conduct herself properly so that if the daughter fails to do this, the blame will not fall on her mother. She first offers advice on deportment. A woman should have a certain hauteur in her manner, yet she should maintain her modesty. She should have a temperate, meek spirit and know how to defer to those who should be honored. She should have a steady gaze and not turn to the left and right, which is a sign of unstable character. The mother states that she learned these precepts at court. It is not enough to have good intentions and to be well instructed, for character is revealed through actions. It is necessary to have self-control and to restrain one's passions, particularly in love.

The attitude toward love is quite different from the one found in the French works, where romantic love is treated only in the context of adultery or flirtation. Here, romantic love is considered a powerful force that can exist inside or outside of marriage. It is regarded seriously and idealistically, not at all in the context of coquetry. The mother strongly recommends honorable love (*hôhe Minne*) but warns against uncontrolled passion (*twingende Minne*). A woman must be careful, for it is difficult to distinguish the good men from the bad, and many men are skillful deceivers. It is best to love a worthy man of one's own rank and to establish an honorable relationship (in terms of medieval morality, marriage). The mother discusses the nature of love and how it can cure or wound hearts, citing Ovid as an authority. *Hôhe Minne* does not abase people but elevates them and enters only into noble hearts. The mother ends by giving several precepts that make a woman worthy of love. She must not envy other women and must be agreeable, chaste, and courteous in all her actions. This work shows the influence of Ovid and courtly love; however, it elevates the emotion, treating it much more seriously than the French works, and domesticates it, making it compatible with marriage. The more serious attitude toward love found in this work has much in common with the one found by W. T. H. Jackson in Middle High German literature.[27]

The *Dodici avvertimenti che deve dare la madre alla figliuola quando la manda a marito*, written about 1300, purports to be a set of instructions from an Italian mother to her daughter when she was about to be married.[28] The mother bids goodbye to her daughter, telling her she loves her and wishes her happiness. She sets forth her advice in the form of twelve precepts, most of them concerning how to get along with a husband. The first is to avoid anything that might annoy him; do not be joyful if he is sad, or sad if he is joyful. Try to find out the dishes he prefers; and if your taste does not agree with his, do not let him see it. If your husband is asleep, sick, or tired, do not disturb him; if you must do so, do it gently. Do not rob your husband, lend his goods, or give them away. Do not be too curious about his affairs; but if he confides in you, keep his secrets. Be good to his family and friends. Do not do anything important without seeking his advice. Do not ask him to do impossible things or things that would damage his honor or position. Be attractive, fresh, clean, and modest in appearance, and chaste in behavior. Do not be too familiar with servants. Do not go out too often; the man's domain is outside, whereas the woman's is in the home. Do not speak too much, for silence is a sign of modesty and chastity. Finally and most important, do not make your husband jealous. The writer of this treatise was aware of a woman's need to placate an irate husband on many occasions.

A poem known as the *The Good Wife Taught Her Daughter* is written in first person as an address from mother to daughter. The oldest manuscript dates from about 1350. Tauno Mustanoja, the editor, believes that it was written by a male cleric;[29] however, the style is not that of a clerk. The poem has a rough rhythm, simple rhyme scheme, Anglo-Saxon vocabulary, and a popular, proverbial tone. Each stanza contains two couplets and a concluding proverb. The next-to-last stanza contains the line, "Now have I taught thee doughter, so dide my moder me."[30] The poem may represent the traditional lore that a mother passed on to her daughter, put into written form or dictated to a scribe by a woman with some literary skill. If it was written by a man, he effectively assumed the persona of a woman of the lower middle-class.

The poem offers religious, moral and practical advice. It begins with religious instruction. The girl is told to love God and the Church and to attend services as often as possible. Women sometimes used going to church as a pretext for getting out to have a good time. The mother exhorts her daughter to attend church with serious intentions, pay attention to the service, and not gossip with friends or family or make fun of people. She should willingly make her offering and pay tithes.

The ideal of behavior set forth for the middle-class girl equals in modesty the one set forth for the lady. She is told to walk in a slow, dignified manner, taking small steps, not moving her body excessively, and keeping her gaze straight ahead. A considerable number of precepts concern her language, which should be modest and reserved. She should not talk too much or too loudly, not laugh too much, neither jest nor swear, not be a scold, and not mock people. When she visits other women, she should not gossip or reveal secrets.

The ideal of dress is one of modesty, frugality, and practicality. She should wear plain work clothes during the week and save her good clothes for Sunday and holidays. She should not wear expensive gowns and garlands in imitation of the dress of a lady, or compete with the rich attire of neighbors. She should be frugal and should not make her husband go into debt by spending too much money on clothes.

The statements made in the poem indicate that the mother and daughter lived on the outskirts of a town, and that they made cloth for sale and possibly brewed ale. The mother tells her daughter not to go to town on the pretext of selling cloth or conducting business when her real purpose is to amuse herself. When she goes to town on business or to do marketing, she should return home as soon as she has accomplished her errand. She should neither gad about visiting friends nor attend wrestling or shooting matches. The mother tells her daughter to stay out of taverns but does not forbid drinking. Whether she serves ale herself or is served, she should drink in moderation.

> If thou be in any stede ther good drynke is alofte,
> Whethir thou serue or sitte softe,
> Mesurely take theroffe, that the falle no blame:
> If thou be ofte dronken, it fallith the to grete scham.
>> That mesure loueth and skill
>> Ofte hath his wille,
>> My leue child.[31]

The statement about serving drinks suggests that the mother expected her daughter to brew ale. Many women of the lower middle-class did so to make extra money, and it was considered a respectable occupation.

The mother tells her daughter how to behave with men. She should not speak to strange men on the street. If a man asks her to marry him, she should answer him sweetly but not make a commitment. Parents were concerned about such commitments made in private because the church considered them binding, even if they were kept secret. The girl should consult with her family about the advisability of the marriage and follow their advice. She should not remain alone with a suitor or accept gifts.

A good deal of advice is given regarding behavior with one's husband. It is most important to be obedient.

> What man the wedde schall befor God with a rynge
> Honour hym and wurchipe him, and bowe ouer all thinge.
> Mekely hym answere and noght to haterlynge [sharply]
> And so thou schalt slake his mod and be his derlynge.
>> [mood = anger]
>> Fayre wordes wratthe slakith,
>> My der child.[32]

A woman should always speak gently to her husband and not show anger, even if he is angry himself. Her disposition should be sweet and cheerful. She should be loyal in word and deed and avoid any action that might damage her reputation.

Advice is also given regarding bringing up children. The lower middle-class woman had to assume this responsibility herself and would not have had a full-time nurse or governess. The mother tells her daughter to teach her children to be humble and obedient. Both wives and children were supposed to practice these virtues. She should not coddle her children but should beat them when they misbehave. "Spare the rod and spoil the child" was the medieval philosophy of child-rearing.

The mother tells her daughter that if she wishes to prosper, she must be a prudent, thrifty housewife. She should not borrow from others and should take good care of her own possessions. She should supervise her servants and the workers in the house to see that they do their work diligently. Her manner toward them should be neither too harsh nor too familiar. Each day she should assign the tasks that are to be done. It is particularly important to see that the workers are not idle when her husband is away. Since artisans lived usually behind or above their shops and their apprentices lived with them, the author probably had these workers in mind as well as domestic workers in making the above statements. As wife and mistress of the household, the daughter should assist with the work herself to set a good example. The treatise sets forth a no-nonsense ideal of diligence, thrift, and prudence for the housewife of the lower middle-class.

The Good Wyfe Wold a Pylgremage is similar in content, form, and setting to *The Good Wife Taught Her Daughter*, which suggests the author may have known the latter work. The one surviving manuscript was copied in the second half of the fifteenth century, but the poem could be earlier. *The Good Wyfe Wold a Pylgremage* is also ostensibly a book of instruction from mother to daughter. In this case, the mother states that she wishes to instruct her daughter before setting out on a pilgrimage.

The mother tells her daughter not to run about from house to house, or young men might try to seduce her. She should not be too familiar with men and should not remain alone with them. To warn her about the danger inherent in such situations, the mother uses the "fire and tow" proverb used by Chaucer in the speech of the Wife of Bath regarding sexual attraction between men and women.

Take hede to thi byssenis, and make not out of sesson.
Syt not witt no man aloune, for oft in trust ys tressoun.
Thow thou thenk no thenke amyse, yett feyr wordys be
  gayssoun [unproductive]
Feyr and towe ileyde togedor, kyndoll hit woll, be resson.[33]

The daughter is told to be modest in dress and behavior and not to
wear expensive, flashy, or revealing clothes, especially skirts that
expose her legs.[34] She should be temperate in eating and drinking
and should not talk too much, jest, swear, or gossip. She should not
gad about in town going to mystery plays, churches, and taverns.
The verbal similarities between this poem and some lines in the
Wife of Bath's Prologue suggest that Chaucer may have known the
poem; however, the similarities involve proverbial language and
situations common in the lives of middle-class women, so it could
be a matter of the same things coming up in the same contexts.

The Thewis [customs] *of Gud Women* contains the same ideal of
modesty, humility, thrift, and prudence, although it is in the form
of a general treatise of instruction for middle-class women rather
than a direct address from mother to daughter.[35] It is written in the
Northern dialect, and the two surviving manuscripts date from the
late fifteenth century. The author states that the good woman should
be restrained in her speech. She should not speak too much, laugh
loudly, jest, swear, or gossip with her neighbors. She should have a
gentle disposition and should not show anger. She should dress in
simple, practical clothing and should not use makeup or dye her
hair. If she pays too much attention to her appearance, people will
think she is in love. She should not flirt with men, whisper with
them in private, or receive messages or gifts from suitors. She should
be loyal, devoted, and obedient to her husband, give her children
moral instruction, and see that they learn a trade so they will be
able to support themselves. The good housewife remains at home
taking care of her household. She does not flit about town or visit
her friends, and does not attend mystery plays or go on a pilgrimage.
The repetition of these "do nots" in the three poems suggests that
visiting friends in town, attending plays, and going on pilgrimages
were among the favorite amusements of middle-class women.

Christine de Pizan addresses women of all social classes in the
Livre des trois vertus, written about 1405. Book I is mainly for the

queen or princess. One of Christine's first bits of advice to the princess is how to live peaceably with her husband. Unlike other parts of Book I, this section is addressed to all women. This approach acknowledges the predominance of a woman's role as a wife. Christine states that if women do not try to live in harmony with their husbands, they will experience the torments of hell. For the preservation of peace, she recommends humility and obedience. A woman can try to influence her husband by charm and gentleness, but she must always obey him, even if she disagrees with him. She must patiently accept his expressions of anger and never express anger herself. Christine encourages women to practice humility, obedience, and patience out of their own sense of dignity rather than out of fear and subservience.

A woman should be concerned with the body and soul of her husband. She should frequently pray for him and give alms in his name. If she is aware of any sin that he has committed, she should talk to his confessor, suggesting that he admonish him, rather than taking it up with her husband herself. She should consult with his doctors about his health and help him to follow good habits. To maintain a comfortable, well-ordered household, she should diligently supervise the work of her servants and participate in the work herself.

A woman should be loyal and faithful to her husband. When people criticize him, she should defend him even if he is wrong. She should not flirt, nor be familiar with other men—in short, never give him any cause for suspicion. If her husband flirts with other women, she should not be jealous. Christine recognizes the existence of a double sexual standard, but unlike most male authors, she does not condone male infidelity. She acknowledges its existence and the fact that wives have to cope with it. She believes a wife deals with it best by being patient and displaying her own virtue. Eventually, this may make a man realize the value of his wife and make him want to give up his mistress.

A woman should hospitably receive her husband's friends and relatives. If she does not like some of them or is bored by them, she should be sure not to show it. She should treat his relatives even better than her own and speak well of them to avoid any disagreement. If her husband should quarrel with them, she should do all she can to reconcile them. She should follow this course of action not only with her husband's relatives but also with his friends and associates.

Christine realizes that many husbands do not merit such treatment, but she defends it on moral and practical grounds.

> If there are some who might perchance reply that we are telling only part of the story, which is to say that we insist that women should always love their husbands and show their love, whereas we do not say whether men always deserve to be so well treated by their wives, as it is well known that some husbands conduct themselves abominably, showing very little love for their wives, or none at all, we reply to this objection that our doctrine in this present treatise is not addressed to men, however much they might need to be instructed. As we are speaking to women alone, we intend to provide them with remedies which may be useful in avoiding dishonor, and thus we advise them to follow the path of virtue, whoever may choose to do the contrary and whether it profit them good or ill, for even supposing that the husband were marvellously perverse in his morals, rude, whatever his background, and ungracious to his wife, or involved with another woman, or with several, the good judgement and the prudence of a wise woman is manifest, whoever she may be, when she knows how to bear all this and to dissemble, without appearing to be aware of anything or showing that she observes anything unusual. For indeed, even if it is all true, there is nothing she can do about it, and she may well reflect to herself: If you speak to him harshly, you will gain nothing, and if he mistreats you, you are heading into a storm. Perhaps he might send you away, and then people would gossip all the more, thus adding to the shame and the disrepute of the situation, or even worse might overtake you. You are obliged to live and die with him, whatever he may be.[36]

A woman demonstrates her own integrity by acting virtuously, no matter what her husband might do. In any event, she must show forbearance since she is tied to him, and marriage is the only "career" open to her.

Christine shows more concern for children than the male authors who deal with the role of the wife. She believes that even though tutors and governesses tend to the daily needs of children in wealthy families, a mother should become personally involved in their upbringing. She should visit them in their rooms when they get up in the morning, when they go to sleep at night, and while they are studying, and supervise their education. Boys should study Latin, the sciences, and politics. Girls should learn to read and study religious and moral treatises. Christine describes the education she considers appropriate for daughters.

> The princess will also wish that when her daughter has reached a suitable age she will be taught to read, and after that she will learn her Hours and her prayers. She will then be given devotional books describing virtuous behavior, but by no means will she be allowed to read of vain things, of folly or of loose living. Such books will not be allowed in her presence, for the learning and teaching that a child experiences in her early youth she usually retains all her life.
>
> Thus the wise mother will give great attention to the upbringing and instruction of her daughters, and as they grow older she will especially be careful, keeping them by her side most of the time, making sure that they respect her. Her own virtuous bearing will thus be an example to her daughters to conduct themselves in a similar manner.[37]

The emphasis is on moral instruction. Christine's own education was much broader since her father taught her Latin, philosophy, and various sciences. In the *Cité des dames*, composed about 1405, Dame Reason utters the opinion that girls would learn as well as boys or even better if they received a similar education.

> I saye to the agayne and doubte neuer the contrary that yf it were the custome to put the lytel maydens to the scole and sewyngly were made to lerne the scyences as they do to the man chyldren, that they sholde lerne as parfytely, and they sholde be as wel entred in to the subtyltes of al the artes and scyences as they be, and peraduenture there sholde be mo of them, for I haue touched here tofore by

> howe moche that women haue the body more softe than
> the men haue, and lesse habyle to do dyuers thynges, by
> so moche they haue the vnderstandynge more sharpe there
> as they apply it.[38]

Dame Reason suggests here that the intellectual potential of girls is
being wasted, and implies that boys and girls should receive the
same education. In the *Livre des trois vertus*, however, Christine is
more conservative. She accepts the actual position of women in
society and recommends an education that will prepare them for it.

Anne of France expresses similar attitudes in the *Enseignements
à sa fille Suzanne de Bourbon*. She wrote the work for her daughter
when Suzanne was fifteen, shortly before her marriage to Charles de
Bourbon in 1505, and presented it to her as a New Year's gift in
1504 or 1505. Suzanne recognized the value of the book for other
women and had it published in 1521.[39] This work falls slightly
beyond my cut-off date of 1500, but it will be included because of
the scarcity of works by known women authors. Anne used Christine's *Livre des trois vertus* as a source. There were two copies of it in
her library as well as a copy of the *Cité des dames*.[40] This alone,
however, probably does not account for the similarities in their
works. Christine and Anne were kindred spirits. Like Christine,
Anne wanted to give women a sense of their personal worth. Her
main concern was how to maintain personal integrity in a corrupt
world. She did not believe in a "cloistered virtue" but saw the value
of being tested. She compared an untested virtue to a castle that has
never been besieged. How can one know its strength? Virtuous
women know how to live morally and chastely in the midst of
temptation.

Anne begins with religious instruction, basing this part of her
work largely on the *Enseignements à sa fille Isabelle* by Saint Louis,
Anne's great-grandfather. Louis favored the contemplative life, whereas
Anne favored the active, moral secular life. The shift illustrates the
changing attitudes of the Renaissance. Like Saint Louis, Anne exhorts her daughter to love and fear God. She should always keep in
mind that she must die and will be rewarded or punished according
to how she has lived.

Anne advises her daughter to do all she can to preserve a good
marriage. She should not be frivolous or bold since boldness suggests

lack of chastity and should avoid familiarity with men other than her husband. Anne emphatically warns her daughter against extra-marital love affairs. She states that many men are boastful deceivers, and a woman should not believe their oaths. Any declarations of love should be refused sweetly but firmly.

Anne gives considerable attention to the speech appropriate for a lady. She should be modest and dignified, talking neither too much nor too little. Being a good conversationalist is an important skill for a woman. She should not engage in gossip or mockery and should be gracious and humble to everyone, particularly her husband.

> Now consider, my daughter, since thus it is, that you who are a weak feminine creature must take pains, whatever good fortune you may have, to conduct yourself graciously in perfect humility, especially toward your lord and hus-band, to whom, after God, you owe perfect love and obedience; and you cannot humble yourself too much with him, nor grant him too much honor; and you must serve him in all his needs, and be sweet, congenial, and amiable to him, and also to his relatives and friends, each one according to his position.[41]

Anne advises her daughter to be good to her husband's family but also tells her not to neglect her own and not to become proud because of her husband's rank.

If her marriage is bad, Anne tells her daughter to bear her problems with patience.

> If you should find yourself in a hostile or unpleasant mar-riage, do not become sad or distressed; but you must praise God and believe that he is just and that he never does anything that is not reasonable. Then, my daughter, if it should be your misfortune to suffer a great deal, have perfect patience, placing all at the will and good pleasure of the Creator.[42]

She should hide her husband's faults, keep his secrets, and should not show jealousy even if he gives her cause. Once again, a woman's virtues are supposed to compensate for a man's faults. The predomi-nant message that Anne conveys to her daughter is to preserve her marriage at any cost.

Like Christine, Anne gives considerable attention to a woman's responsibilities as a mother. She should carefully choose the guardians and teachers of her children and teach them herself to be moral and religious. A mother should dress her daughters sensibly, without great pomp and expense, and should not compete with them but age gracefully. The virtue of her children should be more important to her than their wealth and social advancement.

Although Anne and Christine set forth the same social ideal as the male authors who addressed treatises to wives, they show more sympathy for a woman's point of view and have more to say about the faults of husbands. In their discussions of extramarital love, they give fewer warnings about sacrificing chastity and more about the deceits of men who try to seduce women. Chastity was less of a concern for them since they saw women as temperate by nature. They had more confidence in the virtue of women and believed that they should not be guarded or protected but given responsibility for themselves.

Rather than wanting to lock ladies up within a tower, they wished to extend their sphere, which can be seen in the way they defined a woman's domain. The male authors wished to maintain the patriarchal family structure, with the power in the hands of the men and women acting as useful servants. Christine and Anne accepted the patriarchal family structure but wished to define a woman's role within it broadly and to give women as much freedom and responsibility as possible. Therefore, in their courtesy books they define a woman's domain in an expansive way and reveal liberal social attitudes.[43]

Most of the courtesy books written by male authors define a woman's domain in a confining way and have restrictive social attitudes. Saint Louis defines a woman's domain as the household and the church. Robert of Blois portrays women in a wider range of social settings, but his vision is limited since he sees them mainly as facilitators of sociability. The Knight of the Tower wished to confine his daughters to the family chateau as much as possible. Although he allowed for an occasional celebration, he advised them not to go to jousts, dances, and parties, and to live at home simply and frugally. Similarly, the Spanish father who wrote the *Castigos* also wished to keep his daughters within the home and exhorted them to stay away from games, jousts, and bullfights. Although the

Ménagier de Paris saw part of his wife's domain as the church, the homes of friends, and the streets of the city, he believed that her main place was her own home, where she should care for her husband's property and person.

Barberino's definition of a woman's domain in the *Reggimento e costumi di donna* depends on the social class he is addressing. For women of the upper class, he is very restrictive. He states that a girl of noble rank must be guarded carefully because she sets an example for many. She should attend social events as infrequently as possible. He does not even recommend frequent attendance at church. It is better to have a private altar and to pray at home. When at home, women should stay away from balconies and windows, where they may get the wrong kind of attention. Barberino allows a wider sphere of action for the middle-class girl. He portrays her walking in the street, riding, and dancing and singing in public. Nevertheless, her main place is the home. A still wider sphere of action is provided for female artisans and shopkeepers. Barberino is one of the few authors to portray woman workers in their various domains. He describes woman hairdressers caring for male and female clients, bakers in their shops, fruiterers at their stands, weavers at their loom, millers at the grindstone, and dairymaids distributing their provisions. The peasant girl's domain is the manor on which she works. She has much freedom of action, but for work rather than play. In her leisure hours, which were few, she had much less supervision than upper-class or middle-class girls. Barberino's treatise suggests that upper-class women led a life of luxury and had a great deal of leisure time, but they were confined within the limited realm of the family domicile much of the time and had to observe strict rules of decorum, particularly in public. More freedom was allowed to women of the bourgeoisie, and even more to the artisan and peasant classes, since there was an economic necessity to use their labor. This impression is confirmed in other treatises written for the middle class, such as *The Good Wife Taught Her Daughter*.

Since Anne of France was writing specifically for her daughter, who was to marry Charles of Bourbon, she deals only with the domain of an aristocratic lady of the court. She defines a woman's role within that sphere broadly, showing her as a ruler and diplomat, not just a socialite and household manager. Anne portrays the princess at court, in public assemblies, and in private quarters.

Since Christine de Pizan was addressing women of all social classes in the *Livre des trois vertus*, she defines woman's domain very broadly. Book I, addressed to princesses and ladies of the court, shows the court as a place of amusement yet also as a place of serious political activity where the princess plays a subordinate but important role. Christine next addresses noblewomen who live on their lands. Their domain is not just the house but the entire estate, which they must run in the absence of their husbands. In addressing women of the middle class, Christine shows how their home lives merged with their work lives: they helped their husbands with their businesses or crafts, trained apprentices, and took over the business when their husbands were absent. Her address to peasant women reveals that in addition to being responsible for traditional household chores, they had to help their husbands with most of the labor on the family farm. Women of the lower-middle and peasant classes operated in the domain of men out of economic necessity. Christine gives the most realistic picture of the lives of women in the *Livre des trois vertus*. Being a wife was indeed the most important role for a medieval woman. But in that preindustrial society, people's work lives and home lives were much closer together. In becoming a wife, a woman assumed many other roles in the political and economic spheres. The nature of those roles depended on her rank in society.

V

Woman as Ruler

The queen occupied the most prominent social position during the Middle Ages. Her position was dependent, for by definition she was the wife, mother, or widow of a king. She became a queen at her coronation and held the title of royalty until her death. While her husband was alive, she bore children, managed the royal household, traveled with the court from castle to castle, appeared beside the king on ceremonial occasions, and engaged in a wide range of charitable activities. Her years of widowhood were usually spent upon her dower lands, but she might be called upon to assist her son or to act as regent. In every phase of her career, she played an important part in the public affairs of the realm. During the early feudal period, when institutions were relatively undefined, the queen reigned as a partner with her husband. During the later Middle Ages, however, when the machinery of government became more complex, the political power of the queen waned. She was removed more to the private sphere, and her governmental functions became mainly symbolic. In her study of queenship in Capetian France from 987 to 1237, Marion Facinger has found that during the tenth and eleventh centuries, the intimacy of court life made it possible for the queen to play a major role in government. The court was small and itinerant, governmental functions were undifferentiated, and the physical center of administration was the hall or common room, where the king, queen, and court ate, slept, and ruled. Under these circumstances, the queen could share every aspect of her husband's suzerainty except the military campaigns. Such were the conditions from 987 through the first quarter of the twelfth century.[1]

The fullest expansion of the office of the queen occurred during the reign of Adelaide of Maurienne (1115-37), wife of Louis VI. Although growing and tending toward a division of functions, the court was still compact enough to allow the queen full participation in all of its activities. Like earlier queens, Adelaide shared in the dispensation of justice by acting as a participating member of the *curia regis*, the king's court of justice. In addition to doing the things her predecessors had done—sharing in benefactions to churches, confirmations of donations made by other parties to religious establishments, ecclesiastical appointments, settlements of cases brought before the king's court—Adelaide shared in new extensions of the royal authority. For the first time royal acts included the queen's regnal year along with that of the king. Her name appeared with Louis VI on charters granting royal protection to monasteries and churches, on charters granting communal privileges to towns in the realm, on charters dealing with serfs, and on charters granting special privileges—the right to hold a fair, free use of royal mills, freedom of a city. In addition to Adelaide's participation in the more formal administrative activities of the government as illustrated in the royal charters, she shared in the executive and policy-making functions of the crown. She issued safe-conducts in her own name and joined Louis in his oath of allegiance to Pope Innocent II against the antipope Anacletus. Adelaide was the first queen to possess and use a personal seal.[2]

The development of the apparatus of government, which occurred during the reign of Louis VI and Adelaide, led to a decline in the political power of the queen. Most significant was the growth of a permanent group of advisers around the king and the gradual bureaucratization of the government. While the king and queen still shared the royal power theoretically, the ill-defined role of the queen was vulnerable to change. The partnership had always been an unequal one, with the king as the dominant member and the queen possessing power only because she was his wife.

Beginning with the reign of Louis VII and Eleanor of Aquitaine, the queen's official position declined. This may seem surprising since Eleanor was said to have exerted a strong influence over Louis, but her influence was due to force of personality rather than political power. The queen could continue to affect governmental policy through her influence over her husband, but she was no longer considered his partner, and her name gradually disappeared from royal acts and charters. Eleanor's name appears as assenting to an act on only three royal charters dealing with matters outside Aquitaine for the fifteen years of her reign. This contrasts with the records of Adelaide's reign, which document in twenty-two years ninety-two acts containing the queen's assent, seal, or regnal year.[3]

The queen's official position, which had formerly been a ruling partnership with the king, changed abruptly in the middle of the 1100s. By the close of the twelfth century, the office of the queen had assumed its ultimate shape. All pretense of partnership had been abandoned, and the queen was no longer granted any official status in the government of the kingdom. She still had the prerogative to sit in on the *curia regis*, but her presence was neither expected nor required. The loss to the queen of formal political function did not mean, however, the loss of all function significant to the monarchy. As the prestige and power of the monarchy increased, her social and symbolic roles became more important. A more elaborate coronation ceremony, an increasingly autonomous and extensive household, and a personal seal all added to the prestige of the queen. But she was regarded mainly as the wife of the ruler, the companion of the king in the performance of regal rites. In the following centuries, the main role of the queen was enacted in the social realm. She participated in government on an informal basis since she was able to affect policy through her personal influence over the king. If she was acting as regent for a minor or an absentee king, she could exercise political power directly, but this was the result of unusual circumstances.

The tendency to limit the power of the queen is reflected in the lack of political literature written for her. Her position was first defined theoretically when her role was no longer powerful politically. A mirror for the princess does not appear until the late thirteenth century, and even after that, there are very few. This is in sharp contrast to mirrors for the prince, of which there is a steady stream throughout the Middle Ages.[4] Among the better known ones are *The Person of the King and the Royal Minister* written by Hincmar of Rheims at the request of Charles the Bald, *Policraticus* written in 1159 by John of Salisbury at the court of Henry II of England, *On the Training of Princes* written about 1265-66 by Thomas Aquinas for the King of Cyprus (probably Hugh III), and *The Gov-*

ernance of Princes written about 1287 by Egidio Colonna for Philip
the Fair of France.

The first mirror for the princess was written for Jeanne of
Navarre, wife of Philip the Fair. Jeanne was selected as the wife of
Philip because she was heiress to the kingdom of Navarre and the
fief of Champagne. It was the policy of the Capetian kings to gain
territory through prudent marriage alliances.[5] Jeanne had been brought
up at the French court, and the marriage had been arranged before
Philip became heir to the throne; the fact that he was to be the next
king increased its significance.[6] Jeanne married Philip in 1284,
when she reached the legal age of twelve. The king acted as the lord
of Champagne, but he did not annex the fief to the royal domain;
he was careful to have his acts confirmed by his wife, as Countess
Palatine of Champagne and Brie.

Jeanne exercised some power as Countess of Champagne, but
she did not play an active political role as queen. Although Philip
was devoted to her and was willing to help her friends and prosecute
her enemies, he did not take her advice on major decisions. A good
example appears in the way he handled the Inquisition in Languedoc.
Jeanne sympathized with the opponents of the Inquisition. They
hailed her as a "new Esther" (the Jewish wife of the Persian king
Ahasuerus who saved her people from slaughter by Haman), and
gave her expensive presents. At first Philip sympathized with them
himself, but when he went south to investigate the overzealous
behavior of the Inquisitors, he was insulted by the anti-Inquisition
leaders. When he felt that his royal dignity had been affronted and
became disgusted with the anti-Inquisition groups, he forced the
queen to return her presents.[7]

It is unfortunate that Philip neglected Jeanne's advice, for she
was a valiant, virtuous woman. When Henry, Count of Bar, invaded
her county of Champagne, she led the troops that vanquished him
and took him prisoner.[8] She was a patron of learning and literature
whose acts of patronage included the founding of the College of
Navarre at Paris, and the encouragement of Joinville to write the *Vie
de Saint Louis*.[9] Joinville intended originally to record only his personal adventures in the crusade of 1248-54. Jeanne urged him to set
down reminiscences of Saint Louis, his friend and master, which he
did. Unfortunately, she did not live to see the final product since it
was not completed until 1309, four years after her death.[10]

She was the patron for the *Speculum dominarum*, the first mirror for the princess, written by Durand de Champagne, her confessor, before 1305 (the year of her death). It may be that she commissioned this work in an attempt to publicize the importance of the office of the queen and to make Philip give more weight to her advice. He was interested in mirrors for the prince, for Egidio Colonna wrote the *Governance of Princes* at his request about 1287.[11] The *Speculum dominarum* might have been intended as a companion to Egidio's treatise. The work is dedicated to Jeanne, and an illustration on folio one shows her receiving it. She had the work translated into French as the *Miroir des dames*, the form in which it enjoyed its greatest popularity. Another translation, also called the *Miroir des dames*, was made between 1526 and 1531 by a priest named Ysambert de Saint-Léger for Marguerite of France, Queen of Navarre and sister of Francis I, and her daughters. It survives in only one incomplete manuscript.[12]

As confessor to Jeanne, Durand focuses on the spiritual life of the queen. If she had wanted a work that emphasized her political role, she would have been disappointed. He used a great deal of material from the Church Fathers, and since many of their treatises for women say the same things, it is difficult to pin him down to exact sources. He specifically mentions Saint Augustine's letter to Proba and Saint Ambrose's treatise on virginity.[13] Although he was writing for a queen, he insists on the doctrine that a woman should be subject to her husband, citing Saint Paul and Saint Peter as his authorities. He praises the contemplative life symbolized by Mary rather than the active life symbolized by Martha. Although he recognized the need for a queen to be involved in an active secular life, he believed she should devote herself to religion as much as possible.

The treatise is composed of three parts, the first of which is divided into three sections: the human condition of the queen, her honors and responsibilities, and her spiritual state. Section one contains warnings against pride and temptations of the flesh. Durand claims that women are weaker than men and subject to more illnesses. This doctrine regarding the physical inferiority of women goes back to Aristotle. Thomas Aquinas's restatement of Aristotle's opinions in the *Summa Theologica* gave them a new popularity in the Middle Ages.

Section two is the only part dealing with the queen's political role. She must be worthy of the ceremonial titles given to her, such as *praeclarissima, illustrissima,* and *excellentissima.* When she visits her provinces, she must respond to the requests and petitions of her people. She should visit monasteries, hospitals, and leprosariums, and distribute alms to the poor. The injustices of royal officials should be remedied by her acts of mercy. Her reputation for mercy should make her visits a welcome solace to the poor, the oppressed, and the unfortunate. She should be a model of courtesy in dealing with people of all estates. Using her position to perform good works, she should despise worldly honors and seek honor for her soul.

Section three of part one deals with spiritual grace, which is acquired through humility, charity, and repentence. Chastity and sobriety are important virtues for a queen and for any woman. She must be modest in thought, speech, facial expressions, and gestures. She must have a firm and stable will and heart. Besides being virtuous herself, she should teach her children virtuous behavior. This section contains a long discussion of the vices and virtues. Durand's pet vice is laziness, which he says leads to all others. Other vices he singles out for discussion are curiosity, jealousy, anger, envy, loquaciousness, impetuousness, and pride. In his discussion of pride, he tells the queen not to wear overly luxurious clothes.

The virtues are the same as those which appear in mirrors for princes, but there is more emphasis on the theological virtues. In mirrors for princes, the cardinal virtues come first and are discussed in greater detail. In this mirror for the princess, however, the theological virtues of faith, hope, and charity take precedence and are given more attention. Several chapters are devoted to charity. The cardinal virtues of prudence, fortitude, justice, and temperance are then discussed. More importance is placed on chastity here than in works for men: "Chastity is the great honor of women and ladies, the great and virtuous beauty of souls, and the sweet flaming odor of good reputation of which the sage speaks in Ecclesiastes."[14] The emphasis on chastity and the theological virtues renders the moral ideal in this work less secular than it's counterpart found in mirrors for princes. Other virtues discussed include humility, patience, and perseverance. Among the worldly virtues are magnanimity and magnificence, which enable the princess to be a generous patron of the Church and the arts. In discussing the subject of love, Durand classifies different kinds of love. Virtuous love, which should be pursued, includes love of God, relatives, neighbors, fellow Christians, husband, and children. Sinful love, which should be avoided, involves love of riches, worldly honors, and delights of the flesh.

Part two deals with the acquisition of learning by the noble lady. Durand quotes the saying "Roy qui n'est lectres est aussi comme ung asne courones" [A king who is not learned is like a crowned ass], and he applies it to the queen as well as the king.[15] He cites Vegetius's book on chivalry (*De re militari*) regarding the valuable ancient custom of putting precepts in writing to instruct princes, and he feels this should be done for princesses as well.[16] On the question of education, Durand has a progressive attitude. He believes that noblewomen should be well educated. Knowledge helps us to know ourselves and to know others. It is particularly helpful for rulers since it enables them to know their people as well as their adversaries. Moreover, it is a source of honest occupation for leisure hours. Durand recommends that women read the Bible, the Church Fathers, and religious and moral treatises. He does not suggest any classical authors. He apparently expected the queen to know Latin since he wrote the work in that language. Since she had it translated into French, she probably felt more comfortable with her native language or wished to make the work available to a wider audience.

Part three is mainly a religious treatise. Durand concentrates entirely upon the spiritual life of the queen in this section. He divides his material into four "dwellings": the outer dwelling, which is the queen's household; the inner dwelling, her conscience; the lower dwelling, that of the damned; and the upper dwelling, that of the blessed. The queen should conduct herself so that she will avoid the dwelling of the damned and attain that of the blessed. Durand's emphasis on religion and morality creates an ascetic, unworldly view of queenship.

The only other mirror for the princess written before 1500 is Christine de Pizan's *Livre des trois vertus*. It is not strictly a mirror for the princess since it includes advice for women of all social classes; but Book I, the largest section, falls into this category. It is a combination of a mirror for the princess, a treatise on the estates, and a courtesy book. It is dedicated to Marguerite, daughter of John the Bold, Duke of Burgundy. Marguerite was married to Louis of

Guyenne, the French dauphin, in 1404, when she was only eight years old. It was expected that she would eventually be queen of France, but Louis died in 1415, a few weeks after the battle of Agincourt. In accordance with the custom of the time, Marguerite was sent to the French court to be brought up. It was hardly the most suitable place for a young princess, for it was controlled by Charles VI, an intermittently mad king, and Isabelle of Bavaria, an unscrupulous queen who became involved in a love affair with Louis, Duke of Orleans, her husband's younger brother.[17] Christine undoubtedly had Marguerite in mind when she discussed the need to protect the young princess from the influence of bad examples.

Like Durand de Champagne, Christine begins by discussing the religious life of the princess; however, she remains on a more practical level and stresses the active life rather than the contemplative life. She states that the princess should love and fear God and show her love through good deeds. In discussing the temptations that can assail a princess, she portrays a frivolous queen who stays in bed late, lying between soft sheets and surrounded by rich draperies, thinking only of how she can amass more power and treasure. Christine probably was thinking of Isabelle of Bavaria, who was notoriously fond of power and luxury. In portraying a virtuous queen who resists temptation, she probably was thinking of Jeanne de Bourbon, wife of Charles V, whom she had described earlier in her *Livre des fais et bonnes meurs du sage roy Charles V*.[18] Christine then compares the active life with the contemplative life. She states that the contemplative life is closer to perfection, and the religious orders were founded to enable people to pursue such a life. Yet the active life is also worthy if followed with sufficient devotion.

Christine devotes her attention to the princess who chooses the active life. She assumes that the princess will marry and become the wife of a duke or king. One of her most important functions would be as peacemaker between the duke or king and his barons. As an example of a skilled peacemaker and diplomat, Christine mentions Blanche of Castille, mother of Saint Louis, who is mentioned several times in the *Cité des dames*. The queen should spend much of her time performing charitable activities. She should appoint reliable officers who will help her to seek out people in need, including poor widows, unfortunate wives, poor girls about to be married, women in child-bed, students, priests, and members of religious orders living in poverty. Christine was particularly concerned about helping women in need.

Rather than providing a codified set of virtues, as she does in some of her other works, Christine advises the princess to follow an Aristotelian golden mean for all aspects of behavior. She states that sobriety or temperance and chastity are the most important virtues for a woman. Sobriety should be observed in enjoying physical pleasures, in speech, and in appearance. Unlike most male authors, she is not preoccupied with chastity. She states that if a woman is temperate in her behavior, chastity will follow naturally. She has more faith than male authors in the virtue of women and in their ability to govern themselves.

Christine offers a detailed description of a complete day in the life of an ideal princess. She wakes up early and says her prayers. If time permits, she goes to Mass. If she has been given responsibilities for the government of the country, however, she may be excused from going to church. This is likely to happen when her husband is not in the court. Upon leaving the chapel, she dispenses alms with her own hand, thus setting an example for others. She then listens to the requests and petitions of her people. If she is directly involved in governing the country, she attends the council. Christine provides a portrait of the queen in the council chamber.

When all of this has been accomplished, if the lady is involved in the government, as has been mentioned, she will go to the council, on those days it is meeting, and there she will have such presence, such bearing, and such a countenance as she is seated on her high seat, that she will indeed seem to be the ruler of them all, and everyone will revere her as a wise mistress of great authority. Thus she will listen diligently to all that may be proposed, and to the opinion of everyone present; she will take care to remember the principal points of each problem and the conclusions, and she will note carefully which members speak the best. Then with due consideration and the best possible advice, she will take note of which seems to her the wisest and most lively opinion, but she will also give attention to the diversity of opinions, what causes and reasons inspire the speakers, so that in all questions she

will be informed. When the time comes for her to speak
or to reply, according to the circumstances, she will try to
do it so wisely that she cannot be considered simple or
ignorant. And if she can be informed in advance as to
what will be proposed in the council, and if she can be
prepared for important matters by wise advice, it can only
be to her advantage. [19]

When the meeting of the council is over, the queen has her
main meal of the day in the great hall, surrounded by her entourage.
During the latter part of the day she receives visitors to the court.
After having performed her diplomatic duties she retires to her
apartments, where she and her ladies take up handwork or some
"honest amusement." This might include reading, playing a game,
listening to music, or listening to the recitation of a literary work.
In the evening she attends vespers in her chapel. Afterwards she
relaxes in her garden if the weather is warm. She goes again to the
great hall for the evening meal, which is followed by a period of
socializing with her entourage and with visitors. If necessary, she
will receive visitors to discuss business. She ends the day as she
began it, by saying her prayers. Christine's description of a day in
the life of a princess is idealized but realistic. A large part of the
queen's time was taken up with serious business and with ceremonial activities that had important diplomatic functions. Although
most of her functions were social and ceremonial, she could also
participate in the governing of the realm. Christine portrays a queen
who realizes her role to its fullest extent in the religious, social, and
political realm.

Christine advises the queen on how to win supporters and how
to deal with the atmosphere of intrigue that one often finds at court.
She warns the queen that she can expect to find enemies but can
disarm them most easily by pretending not to notice their spite. She
should be gracious to all of her subjects, including the nobility,
royal officials, the clergy, scholars, the bourgeoisie, and the common people. The clergy and men of learning will praise her in
sermons, public discourses, and written works, thus assuring her of a
good reputation. The support of merchants is particularly important
if she should need to make loans.

Christine presents an idealistic view of the queen's relation to the ladies of her court, using a number of religious metaphors. The queen is a shepherd who must watch over her flock. Although a certain amount of luxury is required because of the high rank of the ladies, she should insist on modesty in dress and behavior. Low-cut necklines and exaggerated fashions are to be forbidden. Flirtation between men and women is to be discouraged. The queen should be like a prudent abbess watching over a convent. Christine was being very idealistic in making this statement, for in the Middle Ages it was far more common for a convent to resemble a court than for a court to resemble a convent.

Christine's practical side emerges in her discussion of finances. She states that the princess should not simply rely on her officials but should carefully oversee her own finances. She should supervise her officials and inspect their reports. Bills should be paid promptly to maintain good credit and to avoid causing hardship for others. She should be well informed about the sources of her income and her expenditures. Christine suggests a specific accounting procedure. The princess should divide her income into five parts: the portion she wants to devote to alms and gifts for the poor; the sum she knows to be necessary for the expenses of her household; the amount needed to pay her officers and the ladies of her court; money for gifts to strangers or to subjects who give evidence of particular merit; and a sum to go into her treasury to be used for jewels, gowns, or other apparel. This discussion shows Christine's competence in handling financial affairs. As a widow with three children, a mother, and a niece to support, she had to develop competence in this area. On the basis of her own experience, she believed that a woman should be trained to handle financial matters so that she would not be at a loss if her husband died.

Christine discusses the conduct of a widowed princess. She should act and dress with appropriate solemnity but must not allow herself to become unduly depressed. In order to bring herself through the period of mourning, she should devote herself to looking after her own interests since nobody else will do this for her. She should make sure that her husband's will is executed faithfully. If he did not provide for his children during his lifetime, she should see that his lands and property are divided fairly. She should defend her own property rights boldly and seek good counsel if anyone tries to cheat her. The dowager queen was expected to live on the lands granted to her in her dower. Christine warns the widow that she can expect trouble and delays in the law courts. This discussion reveals Christine's familiarity with a widow's problems. If the widow's oldest son is still a minor, she will have to govern his lands until he is old enough to assume this responsibility. She can do this most effectively by assuming the role of a diplomatic peacemaker, trying not to antagonize any of his barons.

Christine devotes a considerable amount of attention to the situation of a newly married young princess. Medieval princes and princesses were often married when they were only children to solidify political alliances between families. The child-bride was sent to her husband's court, where she would become familiar with the people and customs that would concern her in her future role as duchess or queen. She was thus brought up in a foreign court, far from family and friends. This was the situation of Marguerite, Duchess of Guyenne, to whom Christine dedicated the *Livre des trois vertus*. Since Marguerite was only eight years old and was too young to comprehend much of what Christine said, we can assume that the advice was directed at Marguerite's parents and advisers. Christine states that the men and women in the entourage of the young princess should be chosen very carefully. It is better for the men to be married. The princess's governess must be chosen with particular care. Christine tells the governess how to act to win the obedience and affection of the young princess. She should be firm but gentle. In teaching her, she should be encouraging and not too critical. She should not force her to work too hard at her studies but should mix work with play. In addition to instructing her, she should tell her tales to entertain her. Christine shows a great deal of insight into the feelings of a child, an attitude that is rarely found in medieval literature. Christine thus provides a complete practical guide of behavior for the queen or princess for every stage of her life, from youth to widowhood.

In the *Cité des dames*, Christine deals with the role of the woman ruler in a more imaginative, speculative, challenging way, using the form of the dialogue to raise questions about the power of women. The openness of the dialogue allows her to pose questions that undermine traditional positions. Her rhetorical strategy enables her to do this even more effectively. The narrator in the *Cité des dames* differs significantly from the author. In reality, Christine had won herself a bold reputation for attacking antifeminist literature and for arguing with some of the most prominent intellectuals of the time in the Quarrel of the Rose.[20] The narrator is a meek, humble, insecure woman, almost a parody of the ideal lady, who bursts into tears and is convinced of her own worthlessness upon reading antifeminist literature. The contrast would have amused Christine's audience. At the same time, this persona allowed her to assume a diffident tone and avoid antagonizing her opposition. The challenges usually arise out of the examples of virtuous women she selects, or out of the statements made by the Three Virtues, Reason, Rectitude, and Justice.

The Virtues seem to show the influence of the Italian Renaissance in their character. In her study of the *Livre des trois vertus*, Mathilde Laigle states that Christine's apparitions are more secular and more rational than those of other medieval French writers; they seem to be goddesses and suggest the swarm of Olympian deities of the Renaissance.[21] In a period when humanists were beginning to give importance to the ideal qualities of citizenship, the basic mission of Christine's Three Virtues was to prepare women for citizenship in the City of Ladies. Christine takes the new civic values of the Renaissance, which were thought to be mainly for men, and applies them to women. In the context of a debate on woman's ability to rule, the representation of civic virtues as females becomes more than a literary device; we are forced to consider Reason, Rectitude, and Justice as part of woman's character.

The question of woman's ability to rule is brought up quite early. In chapter eleven of Book I, Christine asks Dame Reason why women are not allowed to rule or hold seats in the courts of justice. Men say it is because they cannot do it, and "woman that sytteth in the place of Justyce gouerneth her shrewdly" [badly].[22] Reason denies the claim of men. Nevertheless, God has ordained certain jobs for men and certain jobs for women, according to their nature.

> He hath gyuen to men body stronge power, and hardy to go & come & speke, and for that these men that haue that nature lerneth the lawes & ought to put them in execucyon, to holde the worlde in the ordre of Justyce. And they be bounde that in case that ony wolde not obey to the lawes established by ryght & reason that they sholde

make them to obeye by force of theyr bodyes and by
puyssaunce of armes & that the women may not do. For
howe be it that god hath gyuen them vnderstandynge yet
they may not vse it in that manere for theyr honeste. For
it were not conuenyent that they sholde goo sewe them in
Jugement as these men done.[23]

Reason thus argues that although women have sufficient intelli-
gence to serve as rulers and judges, their weak bodies and modest
natures make it unsuitable for them to do so. This weak argument in
support of the male establishment was the culturally accepted position. We know physical strength is not needed to rule or judge but
only to enforce the law. Women are modest and retiring only because they are culturally conditioned to be so. Moreover, women
can be physically strong if they train their bodies. Christine allows
Reason's argument to stand at this point, but she demolishes it with
the examples she provides of the Amazons and other women rulers
and warriors.

Christine's ideal society is the kingdom of the Amazons. In the
real world of medieval Europe, women ruled as queens or regents
only in the absence of men. In the utopian world of the Amazons,
however, women ruled and lived independently, totally free from
the influence of men.

Somtyme the royalme of Amosonye was begonne by the
ordynaunce & entrepryse of dyuers women of grete courage whiche despysed bondage so as the hystoryes bereth
wytnesse. And longe tyme by them it was mayntayned
vnder sygnyouryes of dyuers quenes ryght noble ladyes the
whiche they chose themselfe & gouerned ryght fayre and
well, and by grete strengthe maynteyned the lordshyp,
and neuerthelesse thoughe they were of grete myght &
puyssaunce & that in the tyme of theyr domynacyon con-
quered grete parte of the oryent & all the landes nyghe
them put them in drede.[24]

There are several bloodthirsty versions of the legend of the Amazons. According to some accounts, the Amazons killed their husbands; According to Christine, they lost their husbands, brothers,

and kinsmen in war and then decided to live free from the subjection of men.[25]

Christine tells the stories of nine Amazon queens, emphasizing their ability as rulers, their military prowess, and their chastity or virginity.[26] She values virginity not for the sake of physical purity, but because it frees women from the domination of men. In the portraits of the first two Amazon queens, Martesia and Lampedo, she tells how they accomplished the feminization of Amazon society by banishing all remaining men from their midst and proceeded to perform great feats of arms. In the portrait of Sinope, she embroiders on her source, the *Histoire ancienne jusqu'à César*, highlighting the elements of military prowess and virginity and turning Sinope into an accomplished warrior rather than a novice. She makes Penthesilea a virgin by choice rather than a lovesick woman seeking Hector as a mate, once again highlighting her military prowess and virginity. Her continual association of these two qualities suggests that virginity enhances physical strength. Her polemical purpose was to convince women of the value of virginity in allowing them to be independent of men.

Christine uses versions of the legend of the Amazons that allow her to portray them most favorably. For instance, in her version, the war that Hercules and Theseus conducted against the Amazons ends with a peace treaty, whereas in some versions the Amazons are defeated. Christine emphasizes the duration and the success of the reign of the Amazons in her summation.

> Wherfore yf thou wylte take the leysoure to brynge togyder the hystoryes and to calcule the tymes and the nombre thou shalte fynde that this royalme and the lordeshyp of women endured ryght a longe space, and thou mayst note that in al the lordshyppes that hath ben in the worlde whiche by the space of so moche tyme hath endured one shall not fynde more notable prynces nor in more quantyte ne that hath done more notable dedes than were done by the quenes and the ladyes of that realme.[27]

Christine moves from examples of specific queens to generalizations about the abilities of the Amazons as rulers and soldiers.

To show that the Amazons were not unique, Christine provides other examples of women warriors and rulers from legend and

ancient history, including Semiramis, Camilla, Cleolis, and Zenobia.
She emphasizes again the qualities of virginity and martial prowess.
She portrays Zenobia as an ideal virgin-soldier who welcomes the
asceticism and hardship of military life.

> Of this lady was apperynge all her youthe the grete cour-
> age and knyghtly inclynacyon that she had. For as soone
> as she was strengthed there myght no man kepe her but
> that she wolde leue the dwellynge in the townes, closyd in
> palayces, or in royall chambres but to enhabyte the woodes
> & forestes in which places she had her swerde gurde aboute
> her & dartes by grete dylygence to sle the wylde beestes,
> as hertes and hyndes. And after that began to fyght with
> lyons, with beres, and with many other wylde beestes, and
> she assayled them without drede & ouercame them
> meruayllously. This lady helde it for no payne to lye in the
> woodes doubtynge nothynge vpon the harde erthe, in
> hote and in colde, ne it greued her not to trace the strayte
> passages of the forestes, graue vpon the mountaynes, dyke
> in the valays, rennynge after the bestes. This lady dyspraysed
> all carnall loue, & longe tyme refused maryage as she that
> wolde kepe her vyrgynyte, yet at the last constrayned by
> her kynne she toke to housbande the kynge of Palmurenes.[28]

Once Zenobia condescends to accept a husband, she shares all of his
hardships in warfare.

> This kynge of Palmurenes assembled his grete hoost and
> Cenobye made no grete force of the fresshnes of her beaute,
> but dysposed her to suffre the trauayle of armes with her
> housbande, and to were harnoys, & to be partycypant
> with hym in all labours in the exercyse of knyghthode.[29]

Beside being an ideal knight, Zenobia is a scholar. She is learned in
Egyptian, Greek, and Latin and helps to record the history of her
realm. Christine thus portrays in a princess the Renaissance ideal of
the perfect prince.

Christine also uses examples from French history, sometimes
modifying historical facts to suit her polemical purpose of demonstrating the excellence of women as rulers. Her modification of the
portrait of Fredegund is most dramatic. In fact, Fredegund was a

powerful but cruel queen. She was of humble birth and a maid to
Queen Audovera, wife of King Chilperic. She plotted to have her
mistress repudiated and dispatched to a convent, where she had her
murdered. Then Fredegund herself married the king. Whenever she
felt threatened, she did not hesitate to resort to assassination. She
was responsible for the murder of Chilperic's third wife, the Visigoth
princess Galswintha; the assassination of numerous political enemies, including Chilperic's brother Sigebert; the killing of Chilperic's
sons by other wives and concubines; and various tortures and poi-
sonings.[30] Christine quickly glosses over Fredegund's cruelty, not
giving a single example of it.

> Of ladyes of wyse gouernaunce I myght telle the ynoughe.
> The quene of Fraunce Fredegonde that had ben the wyfe
> of kynge Charles notwithstandynge she was cruell out of
> naturall lawe of women, yet after the dethe of her housbande
> she gouerned the royalme of Fraunce by grete prowesse,
> whiche was at that tyme in ryght grete balaunce.[31]

Instead, she portrays Fredegund as a protective mother, a wise ruler,
a clever parliamentarian, and an expert military strategist. In chapter twenty-two of Book I, she shows Fredegund leading her army
and adapting a strategem from Frontinus, which Christine uses later
in her *Book of Faytes of Armes and of Chivalrye*.[32]

Another example from French history used by Christine is that
of Blanche of Castille.[33] In this case, she did not have to distort
history. Blanche was noted for her piety and morality but also knew
how to exercise power. After the death of her husband, she immediately had her son crowned as Louis IX to assert his right to the
throne and hers to the regency. She put down rebellions by Pierre
Mauclerc, Count of Brittany, and Thibaud, Count of Champagne,
using diplomatic means to reconcile her enemies. Blanche was her
son's trusted counselor throughout his reign. After Louis recovered
from a serious illness in 1248, he took an oath to go on a crusade.
Although she was in her sixties, Blanche again had to act as regent.
She died in the midst of her responsibilities while Louis was impris-
oned in the Holy Land.[34] Christine does not give a detailed account
of Blanche's career but provides a general picture of her reign,
asserting that France "was never better governed by man."[35] Chris-

tine moves from the example of Blanche to generalize about the ability of women as regents:

> For be it no doubte nor dyspleasaunce to men that there ben many women that haue better vnderstandynge than some of these men haue, of the whiche yf theyr housbandes had byleued them that they had suche vnderstandynge as they had it myght haue tourned theym to grete profyte.[36]

Their husbands wasted these women's talents by not making use of them while they were alive.

The examples that Christine sets forth in the *Cité des dames* and the generalizations she draws from them have radical implications. They suggest that women indeed have the ability to rule and to "sit in the place of Justice." The only thing that has kept them out of power is their subjugation by men. The kingdom of the Amazons and Christine's own City of Ladies provide examples of women governing themselves effectively, totally free from the domination of men. Since Christine was not a revolutionary, she drew back from this radical vision. In the final chapter of the *Cité des dames*, she advises women to be humble and submissive to their husbands.

> So my ladyes as be it true that the more the vertues ben the more ye ought to yelde you humble & benygne, and this Cyte be cause vnto you to loue good maners, and to be vertuous and humble. And haue ye not in despyteye ladyes that ben maryed to be so subiectes to your housbandes. For it is not some tymes beste to a creature to be free out of subieccyon.[37]

The *Cité des dames* thus ends on a submissive note. Christine does not advocate the emulation of the exploits of heroic women but rather the translation of their virtues into domestic and private terms. In the *Livre des trois vertus*, written immediately after the *Cité des dames*, Christine is conservative throughout the work and provides a practical guide of behavior for women in the real world.

VI

Woman as Worker

Women played an important economic role in the Middle Ages at every level of society. The main task of the aristocratic woman was to supervise the running of her household and her estates. This responsibility made her virtually a business manager, for a manorial household was so large that it was like a business establishment. A list of officials for the barony of Eresby in the last quarter of the thirteenth century gives a good idea of the extent of the household of even a minor baron.[1] There was a steward who was in charge of the estates and a wardrober who was the chief clerical officer and examined the daily expenditures with the steward. The wardrober's deputy, the clerk of the offices, was responsible for writing letters and documents. Although their duties were mainly religious, the chaplain and almoner could be required to help write letters and documents or to act as comptroller. There were two friars, who could substitute for the chaplain, and a boy clerk. The purely domestic servants included a chief buyer, a marshal, two pantrymen, two butlers, two cooks, two larderers (officials in charge of the room where meat was stored), a saucer (a cook who prepared sauces), a poulterer, two ushers, two chandlers, a porter, baker, brewer, and two blacksmiths. These men were assisted by their own boy helpers. Women servants tended the laundry and the kitchen and provided personal services for the lady of the manor.

The household account detailed minutely the way in which money was disbursed. In large households, it was not unusual to have two accounts, one for the lord and one for the lady.[2] Since the lord was often away on business, it was primarily the lady's business to oversee these accounts. A lady of the manor was expected to have a knowledge of the accounting procedures that applied to estate management.She had to know her major sources of income and her major expenditures.

Rents and feudal fees were a main source of income, but on an efficiently run estate, a considerable amount of money could be made from items produced on the demesne lands retained by the lord and lady and not rented out. These products were also used on the manor, which was a partially self-sufficient economic unit. Grain was used to make bread, ale, and fodder for livestock. If there was a surplus, it could be sold at the market. Eggs, butter, milk, and cheese came from animals kept on the manor. Once again, a surplus could be sold for a profit. Animals were slaughtered at appropriate times of the year, and the meat that was not used immediately was salted for consumption during the winter. Most manors had their own fish ponds for fresh fish, but salt fish such as herring had to be purchased. Most of the fruits and vegetables that were used were homegrown. Herbs for cooking and for medicinal purposes came from the garden. Dried fruits, salt, spices, and wines were purchased to enhance the bland diet derived from homegrown foods. Wool from the sheep kept on the manor was sold to merchants or woven into homemade fabrics. Only simple fabrics were made on the manor. The more elaborate, expensive ones were purchased in town and at fairs. The lady of the manor and her servants made many of the everyday clothes worn by members of the household; however, more elaborate garments were custom-made by professional tailors. Items such as shoes, belts, hats, purses, and laces were purchased from artisans. The lady of the manor had to keep control of this flow of goods and maintain adequate supplies for the entire household.

If the lord and lady owned more than one manor, which was common, supplies had to be maintained at each of them. Landowners moved about from manor to manor, transporting their entire household. This was the cheapest way to live when the produce of the land was the chief source of wealth. When the stores and supplies of one manor were exhausted, the owner and his family moved on to another one.[3] The lady of the manor and her officials took charge of moving the household. She was accustomed to riding and arranging the details of a journey.

When her husband was away on business or at court, the lady

of the manor had to supervise the external economy of the manor as well as the household. She had to supervise her workers and tenants, hear their complaints, and even hold a court. To do this she needed a knowledge of feudal and common law. Since knights and barons often engaged in feuds with each other and turned to the sword to solve their differences, the lady of the manor might have to defend her lands while her husband was away. For this purpose, she needed a knowledge of military operations and military law. She had to act as her husband's business agent while he was away and do things such as pay or collect debts, collect rents, and negotiate agreements, all the while carrying on an extensive correspondence to keep him informed of her actions. Such collections as the Paston Letters and the Stonor Letters bear witness to the business ability of medieval women.[4] The managerial skills of women freed men to engage in wars, crusades, politics, and commerce, activities that led to the geographical expansion of Europe.[5]

Middle-class women were expected not only to maintain their households, which were usually town houses within the city, but also to assist their husbands in business. A woman could be of assistance to her husband by helping him in his trade or by practicing one of her own. She could trade as a *femme sole* even if she were married, provided her husband did not interfere in her business. In such a case, she could rent a shop of her own. She alone was responsible for anything concerning the practice of her craft. If she were sued in court, she could plead as a *femme sole*, and her husband would have nothing to do with the case. If she were condemned to make payment, she would be committed to prison until she made a settlement with her creditors, her husband remaining entirely untouched in person and property. If a married woman did not trade as a *femme sole*, she could plead coverture, and then her husband was responsible for her debts and misdeeds.[6] A married woman in business had a legal advantage over a man since she could either take full responsibility for her actions or place that responsibility upon her husband. After 1363, married women in London had another advantage over men, for an act passed in that year ordered men to keep to one trade, whereas women were left free to follow as many as they chose.

In the merchant class, married women often carried on trades even if there was no economic necessity for them to do so. It was a way to keep busy and to earn extra spending money for luxuries. In London, a fishmonger's heiress who was married four times engaged herself in tailoring and brewing. A fishmonger's widow bequeathed to a male apprentice all the equipment from a metal working shop she had directed. Dame Elizabeth Stokton had cloth manufactured for export to Italy.[7]

Margery Kempe was the daughter of an alderman of Lynne and the wife of one of the town's wealthiest merchants, yet she took up brewing ale and grinding corn in a horsemill. She reports in her autobiography that she did not have success with either of these activities (Margery speaks of herself in third person even though she was dictating her own life story to her scribe). When she tried to brew ale, the barm (the froth that forms on the top of fermenting ale) always fell.

> And than, for pure coveytyse & for to maynten hir pride, sche gan to brewyn & was on of the grettest brewers in the town N. a iii yer or iiii tyl sche lost mech good, for sche had neuyr vre [success] thereto. For thow she had neuyr so good seruawntys & cunnyng in brewyng, yet it wold neuyr preuyn wyth hem. For whan the ale was as fayr standyng vndyr berm as any man mygth se, sodenly the berm wold fallyn down that alle the ale was lost euery brewyng aftyr other, that hir seruawntys weryn aschamyd & wold not dwellyn wyth hir. Than this creatur thowt how God had punched [punished] hir be-for-tyme & sche cowd not be war, and now eftsons be lesyng of hir goodys, & than sche left & brewyd no mor.[8]

Rather than abandoning the pursuit of material wealth, she rented a horse mill and hired a man with two horses to grind corn; but the horses would not draw, no matter what the man did.

> But yet sche left not the world al hol, for now sche be-thowt hir of a newe huswyfre. Sche had an hors mille. Sche gat hire tweyn good hors & a man to gryndyn mennys corne & thus sche trostyd to getyn hir leuyng. This provysion duryd not longe, for in schort tyme aftyr on Corpus Cristi Evyn fel this merueyl. Thys man, beyng in good heele of body & hys tweyn hors craske & lykand [lusty and in good

condition] that wel haddyn drawyn in the mylle be-for-
tyme, as now he toke on of this hors & put hym in the
myle as he had don be-for, & this hors wold drawe no
drawt in the mylle for no-thing the man mygth do. The
man was sory & asayd wyth al hys wyttys how he schuld
don this hors drawyn. Sum-tyme he led hym be the heed,
sum-tyme he beet hym, & sum-tyme he chershyd hym,
and alle avayled not, for he wold rather gon bakward than
forward. Than this man sett a scharp peyr sporys on hys
helys & rood on the hors bak for to don hym drawyn, & it
was neuyr the bettyr. Whan this man saw it wold be in no
wey, than he sett up this hors ageyn in the stabyl and gafe
hym mete, & he ete weel & freschly. And sythen he toke
the other hors & put hym in the mylle. And lech as hys
felaw dede so dede he, for he wold not drawe for any-thing
that the man mygth do. And than this man forsoke hys
seruyse & wold no lengar abyden wyth the fornseyd creatur.[9]

Margery attributed her lack of success to her worldliness and pride;
she wanted to be the richest and best dressed woman in town and
confesses that "sche had ful greet envye at her neybowrs that thei
schuld ben arayd so wel as sche."[10] When her husband criticized her
for her pride, she retorted by boasting about being the daughter of a
mayor and an alderman and stating that her husband was of too low
a rank to deserve her.

> And whan hir husband wold speke to hir for to leuyn hir
> pride, sche answeryd schrewydly & schortly & seyd that
> sche was comyn of worthy kenred, hym semyd neuyr for to
> a weddyd hir, for hir fadyr was sum-tyme meyr of the town
> N. and sythyn he was alderman of the hey Gylde of the
> Trinyte in N.[11]

Margery states that in order to punish her for her pride, God caused
her enterprises to fail.

Margery's worldliness, ambition, and pride were common qualities among women of the middle class. The wives of aldermen
insisted upon the title of "lady," which was used for the wives of
knights and esquires.[12] The desire for additional wealth motivated
many women to pursue trades of their own. If they were successful

in business, the income they earned was a source of independence, pride, and self-confidence.

Guild records tell us a great deal about the participation of women in trades. In Paris, women engaged in over a hundred trades.[13] Some were practiced only by women. These included the trade of spinner of silk, hatmaker of silk, maker of alms purses, weaver of silk, maker of silk ribbons and kerchiefs, and dresser of hemp and flax. Others were practiced by both men and women, including the trade of embroiderer, hatmaker of pearls, hatmaker of cloth of gold or silver, spinner of fabrics other than silk, weaver of linen, draper, poultry dealer, and chandler. Still others could be practiced by women on their own only if they took over their husbands' businesses as widows. Among these were the trade of apothecary, butcher, metal worker, brewer, maker of felt hats, barber-surgeon, shoemaker, maker of leather goods, maker of knives, worker in precious stones and crystal, fuller, weaver, cook, maker of rosary beads and other beaded work, fish dealer, furrier, tailor, baker, tapestry maker, and dyer. Many of the guilds of Paris do not specify in their ordinances as to whether men and women could practice the trade on equal terms.[14]

In London, no trade was closed to women by law, and evidence exists in civic and guild records for their employment in occupations of many kinds. Women engaged in some of the most important and remunerative trades as mercers, drapers, grocers, and merchants. A number of them were sufficiently prominent as businesswomen to be called upon to serve the king. Henry III paid Mariot, wife of Robert de Ferars, over seventy-five pounds for palfreys, horses, harnesses, and other equipment. He bought lime, hurdles, and poles for his palace at Westminster from women. In 1301, Dyonisia la Rowere provided wheels for the use of Edward I in Scotland. Silkwomen worked for Edward IV and Henry VII.[15]

Women practiced some trades that were later restricted to men. There are records of woman barbers, apothecaries, armorers, shipwrights, tailors, spurriers, and water bearers. They were among the barber-surgeons who practiced surgery along with the regular surgeons and afterwards joined with them to form the Royal College of Surgeons in London.[16] Women also practiced the trade of barber-surgeon in Paris, but they were not allowed to attend the university to become *chirurgiens de robe longue*, that is, surgeons who acquired further medical knowledge by pursuing formal courses, for which they obtained a special license.[17] In Paris, we also find records of women working in the building trades as masons, carpenters, makers of doors, and diggers of gravel.[18] Women worked right beside men in clearing the land and in constructing the foundations of buildings.

The silk industry attracted the largest number of woman workers. Many of the trades in this industry were practiced only by women. They worked as spinners, weavers, and makers of ribbons, kerchiefs, fringes, tassels, laces, girdles, caps, purses, and other small articles of silk. In Paris, women guild members supervised workers in their craft as *jurées*, elected officers sworn to uphold the regulations and standards of the craft; however, they had to be assisted by a husband of one of the *jurées*.[19] The spinners of silk were all women, yet they were supervised by men.[20] The makers of silk ribbons were almost all women, but the six *jurées* had to include three men and three women.[21]

The silkwomen of London were jealous of foreign competition and guarded their interests carefully. In 1368 they delivered a bill to the mayor and aldermen, complaining that Nicholas Sarduche, a Lombard, had been buying all the silk he could find and raising the price of it. In addition, they petitioned the Crown, with the result that a writ was issued ordering the civic authorities to do them justice; an inquiry was made, and Sarduche was found guilty. In 1455 they again petitioned the Crown, declaring that more than a thousand women were employed in the silk industry, and requesting that the importation of similar goods from abroad might be prohibited. An act was passed in accordance with their wishes.[22] The silkwomen were as astute as any male workers in pursuing their political interests.

The woman workers of Paris were engaged in making many luxury items. The *chapelières* made delicate hats meant mainly for decoration. One of their most popular creations was made of *orfrois*, a lacework of cloth of gold or silver. In the spring, they made hats and garlands of flowers. *Mercières* used a base of silk to make hats of peacock feathers, beads, pearls, and precious stones. *Crespinières* made ornaments of thread and silk. *Patenotrières* made rosary beads and other beaded items.[23] The skilled work of these women made Paris an important center for luxury goods.

Women worked as artists, scribes, and producers of manuscripts.

They were members of the guild of illuminators and were skilled painters of miniatures.[24] In the *Cité des dames* Christine de Pizan praises the work of a Parisian illuminator named Anastasia.[25] An artist in London left her apprentice one third of her copies and instruments pertaining to the making of pictures and one of her best chests to hold them.[26] Women also practiced the craft of binding manuscripts. In the accounts of the prisoner King John of France for January 1358, we find the name of Marguerite the binder, who rebound a copy of the Bible.[27]

Women were active in the food trades. This is not surprising since brewing and baking were home industries originally. Men gradually took over the trade of brewing, however, and tried to exclude women. In 1356 when thirty brewers were appointed to serve the king with ale, only one was a woman. In a list of London brewers for the year 1420, less than twenty out of three hundred were women. Nevertheless, many women brewed ale on a small scale, and many kept alehouses and inns. Women engaged in the retail food trade and sold such items as poultry, fish, and bread. There were also woman bakers who ran bakehouses of their own.[28]

In every trade, men could make their wives and daughters apprentices, which accounts for women entering trades where they would not be expected. Husbands and wives frequently worked together, the wife helping her husband when he was at home and acting for him in his absence. They sometimes had apprentices who served them both. Husband and wife were jointly responsible for debts. When a man died, his wife was often capable of continuing his business, and the ordinances of the guilds allowed her to do so. In the wills of craftsmen, we find numerous bequests to their widows of their apprentices' services and the implements of their trades. Such bequests are found for apothecaries, bakers, carpenters, cooks, curriers, drapers, dyers, fishmongers, girdlers, goldsmiths, joiners, mercers, skinners, tanners, and weavers.[29]

The lower down we go on the social scale, the more equality we find in the work that was done by men and women. Peasants, the largest class of working women, were also the hardest working. If they were married, they were expected to share in all of their husbands' labors on the family farm. They engaged in planting, weeding, reaping, binding, threshing, winnowing, and even helped with the plowing. In their own garden they grew vegetables and herbs, and looked after the poultry, pigs, and other barnyard animals. In addition to these agricultural labors, women were burdened with the traditional feminine household chores. They had to spin and weave linen and wool for their own family and sometimes made extra material for sale. Spinning was such a common occupation of peasant women that it was hardly recognized as a specialized craft. Women sometimes worked on yarn brought to them from the towns.[30] Once the material was prepared, they turned it into clothing for their families. Clothes had to be washed and mended, and the house had to be cleaned. Products such as soap and candles were either not for sale or could be purchased only in town or at markets, and so the peasant housewife often made them herself. She served as the family doctor, using ancient charms and herbal recipes to cure her family of common ailments. She baked her own bread, brewed her own ale, made cheese and butter, and cooked for her family.

Unmarried women or widows who possessed holdings in their own name were even more overworked. Women were allowed to hold farms in their own name if they inherited them from husbands or male relatives. Almost every manorial survey lists a few women as free tenants, villeins, or cotters.[31] They had the same obligations as a male tenant and had to render the same services. They owed a certain number of days' labor per week on the lord's demesne as well as extra services at sowing or harvest time, which included helping to cart the products harvested on the manor. They owed a certain number of eggs and chickens per year. In addition to these goods and services, they had to pay certain feudal fees. Payments also could be made in lieu of goods or services. Women usually hired men to do the heavy plowing for them, both on their own land and to fill in for them on the lord's demesne, but they performed the other services themselves.

Whether a peasant woman was married to a free tenant or a serf, her way of life did not differ very much. Regardless of her legal position, she was tied to the soil, and her existence centered around her farm and family. She lived in a cottage on the farm and worked as part of a family unit. The main feudal obligation of the female serf was to spin and weave a fixed quantity of material every year for the lord of the manor. Sometimes it was a piece of linen, called a *camsilis*, and sometimes a piece of wool, called a *sarcilis*. She might also make cloths for the dining table or coverings for the altar. However, she could free herself from this obligation by paying a fixed sum or by donating a certain amount of wine or poultry.[32]

Some peasant women worked directly on the lord's demesne. A few girls of this social class were employed as domestic servants in the lord's household. Women were hired by bailiffs to do every kind of agricultural labor except plowing. Where the hand mill was used, it was often turned by women. Women did most of the shearing of sheep, and they prepared the wool for spinning. They also picked the flax and prepared it for spinning into linen.

All of this economic activity is not reflected in most of the courtesy books of the time. When it comes to the working lives of women, we find a disjunction between image and social fact. It might be thought that it is not surprising for courtesy books to ignore work since their main purpose was to teach manners and morals, but courtesy books for men give a great deal of attention to their occupations and little attention to their domestic lives. Another consideration might be that most of the treatises were written for aristocratic women or wealthy women of the bourgeoisie, the only literate classes. Literacy did not go very far down the social scale. Although Margery Kempe was a mayor's daughter, she was not literate. Most middle-class women who had some degree of literacy could not afford manuscripts, which were a luxury item. Nevertheless, this does not explain fully the lack of attention given to women as workers. The occupations of aristocratic women are neglected as well as those of middle-class women and peasants. As in the case of the woman ruler and her responsibilities within the political realm, there seems to have been a reluctance to portray women's full responsibilities within the economic realm. Most of the courtesy books concentrate on women's role within the home and the familiy. Francesco Barberino's *Reggimento e costumi di donna* and Christine de Pizan's *Livre des trois vertus* are the only works that portray a full range of women's occupations within society.

Francesco Barberino deals with women's economic roles in a rather cursory manner. Although he addresses women of different social classes in the *Reggimento e costumi di donna*, most of his advice concerns their roles as young girls about to get married or as wives. His focus is upon the responsibilities of women within the family. Even when he addresses women as workers, the organization of the *familia*—the large medieval household—dominates his thinking.

Barberino first addresses ladies in waiting.[33] They should love and respect their mistress, taking part in her joys and sorrows and putting up with her anger. They should take care of her belongings, accompany her when she goes out, not be too curious about her secrets, and not flatter her. They should love and respect the children of their masters and lead chaste, honorable lives.

Next come domestics.[34] Women of this class must be very careful if they wish to preserve their chastity. They should not enter the service of an unmarried man, unless they are sure they can trust him. They should not listen to the flattery of young gentlemen and not trust male domestics who work with them. In all of their work, they should be clean, especially in the kitchen. They should be honest and not rob their masters. They should dress plainly and be diligent and frugal to provide for their old age.

Barberino goes on to describe the qualifications and duties of a nurse.[35] She should be between twenty-five and thirty-five years old, strong, sturdy, with good color, firm flesh, and good teeth. Her milk should be white and plentiful so that she will be able to nurse the child for two years. The nurse must know how to swaddle a newborn baby, wash him, sing to him, rock him in the cradle, put him to sleep, comfort him, and teach him to stay away from things that would hurt him. It can be seen that many duties which are now considered maternal were the job of the nurse in the Middle Ages.

The last household workers to be addressed are the serfs and slaves, the most unfortunate since servitude is against human nature.[36] The serf or slave must serve the family of her master with respect, faith, and loyalty. If she learns of any danger to her master, she should immediately inform him of it. She should pray for her master and help him as much as possible. If she demonstrates her loyalty, he may reward her by granting her freedom.

Barberino turns away from the household to address women who exercise different trades.[37] He tells hairdressers to concentrate on their combs and razors, and not on flirting with clients. Bakers should not use false weights, deceive their customers, or allow servants to gossip about their masters in their shops. Fruiterers should not place fresh leaves on old fruit to make it appear fresh, place good fruit on top to hide the bad, or put oil on figs to make them seem ripe. They should not buy bread or wine from servants who have stolen these provisions from their masters. Weavers should not trick customers by giving them a false measure of materials. Millers should not put flour in a damp place or give bad flour in exchange for good grain. Venders of poultry and cheese should not wash their eggs or cheese to make the products appear fresher and should not deceive their customers. Pedlars should not serve as messengers for lovers and should not sell fake jewelry. Beggars also should not convey messages for lovers. If they serve as messengers for a legitimate purpose, they should not pocket the money without delivering the message. They should not resell old bread, curse if someone does not give them alms, or lie when begging. Innkeepers should not serve leftover food as fresh food, give their guests bad food, try to delay their departure, or mistreat their horses. Barberino provides a good idea of the many occupations exercised by women during the Middle Ages. His selection of professions reflects the predominance of women in the food and clothing trades. Rather than taking interest in their actual work, however, he assumes the point of view of a customer who does not want to be cheated.

Like Barberino, Christine de Pizan addresses women of all social classes in the *Livre des trois vertus*; but unlike him, she does not focus on their familial roles. She shows as much interest in their economic roles and recognizes fully their contribution to society within the economic sphere. She is strongly interested in the details of their work and the skills they needed to perform it. For example, she describes the extensive knowledge of law, accounting, warfare, agriculture, and textile production needed by the lady of the manor.[38] The lady who lives on her estates must be wise and must have the courage of a man. This is true because she must represent her husband during his frequent absences. Although he has bailiffs, provosts, and collectors, she must supervise these officials and see that they do not cheat her. In order to do this, she must know the laws and customs of the place, such as the rights of fiefs, the lord's rights of harvest, and feudal fees and penalties. She should see that her officials treat her tenants fairly. In deciding penalties against the poor, she should be compassionate. In order to enforce justice, she must be a good speaker—proud and commanding to those who are surly and rebellious, gentle and charitable to those who are obedient. She should not oppress her tenants and workers but should be

just and consistent. She should follow the advice of her husband
and of wise counselors so that people will not think she is merely
following her own will.

She must know the laws of warfare so that she can command
her men and defend her lands if they are attacked. She must know
how to conduct an assault or a defense. If there are any fortresses on
her lands, she should see that they are in good repair. It is particularly important for her to know how to conduct herself during a
siege, the most common medieval military operation. Before taking
any action, she must know what resources she can call upon.

She should know everything pertaining to her husband's business affairs so that she can act as his agent in his absence or for
herself if she should become a widow. She must know the yearly
income from her estates so that she will not get into debt. It is
important for her to have a good knowledge of accounts, and she
should frequently go over them herself rather than rely on her
steward.

She must be a good manager of workers. She should hire reliable workers and supervisors who do not change jobs too often. The
workers she hires should be neither too old, since old workers tend
to be lazy, nor too young, since young workers tend to be frivolous.
She should hire part-time workers early in the season, in August,
and should not wait until the supply is short. She should insist that
her workers get up early and should arise herself to check on them,
putting on a cloak and going to the window to watch them as they
go out to the fields. She should take her recreation by going for a
walk in the fields to see what her workers are doing, for many might
not rake the ground below the surface or might sleep in the shade of
a willow tree if they think nobody is watching.

To supervise her workers, she needs a good knowledge of farm-
ing. She must know in what weather and in what season the fields
should be worked, the best way to have the furrows run according to
the lay of the land, and the seed that is best suited to the soil. If her
lands are in a winegrowing region, she should know how to cultivate vineyards. She should see that her shepherd cares properly for
her sheep, putting them out to pasture on schedule. The flocks
should be kept clean, cured of the mange, and protected from too
much sun or rain. Newborn lambs must receive good care, and
shearing must be done in the proper season. If she has good lands for

grazing, she will keep many horned animals, a valuable source for food and profit. She will also keep good stables for her horses. She will see that trees are cut down and wood stored at the right time of year. She will make sure that her woman laborers look after the barnyard animals, prepare food for the workers, milk cows, weed the garden, and gather herbs.

She will be sure to have adequate supplies for the spinning and weaving of cloth. She, her daughters, and her servants will sort out the wool, putting aside fine strands to make cloth for herself and her husband and thick strands to be used in garments for children, serving women, and workmen. Large balls of wool will be made into bed covers. She will have hemp grown on her lands to be spun into coarse linen cloth. Christine states that by following these practices, the wise housekeeper can sometimes bring in more profit than the revenue from the land.

Christine next turns to middle-class women. Her warnings to them about indulging in too much luxury bear witness to the wealth of the upper bourgeoisie in Paris in the fifteenth century.[39] She describes the extravagant display at a lying-in for a rich merchant's wife when she gave birth. Before entering the woman's room, one passed through two others, each with a large ornamental bed richly curtained. In the second room there was a large dresser arrayed like an altar, covered with silver vessels. The woman's room was hung with tapestries marked with her coat of arms and worked in fine gold. Her bed was richly curtained and had a coverlet woven in thread of gold. The rugs surrounding the bed were also worked in gold. In the room there was a large dresser covered with gilded vessels. The woman was wearing a crimson silk gown and a head-dress in the style of a lady of the court. She was propped up on crimson silk pillows decorated with pearl buttons. When the extravagance of this event was reported in the Queen's chamber, someone remarked, "The Parisians have too much blood, the abundance of which sometimes brings on certain maladies."[40] The Queen and her ladies would have been offended because the display at lyings-in or baptisms was supposed to be in keeping with the rank of the woman. Christine protests against the foolishness of such a display. When women of the bourgeoisie indulge in extravagant displays of wealth, they merely encourage the king to tax their husbands.

Christine tells women of the middle class to avoid extravagance in their dress. If they are wealthy, it is suitable for them to wear handsome clothes, but they should not imitate the fashions of the upper classes. In buying and ordering clothes, they should not go to extremes in expense or style. Fashions that involve a great deal of excess material, such as long trains and hanging sleeves, are expensive, impractical, and quick to wear out. Modesty should be observed, and designs that are flashy, too tight, or too low-cut should be avoided.

A woman should be discreet about the social events she attends. She should not accept invitations to gatherings arranged by lords, clerics, or other people who use the pretext of entertaining a group of people to conceal some machination with regard to an affair for themselves or others. She should not go on pilgrimage just to have an excuse to travel or to amuse herself out of the sight of her family and neighbors, nor should she wander around the town going to different churches with the pretext of attending services when her main purpose is to have a good time. She should not go to bathing establishments, taverns, and other public places. Christine's admonitions reveal the freedom that was available to middle-class women.

According to Christine, the middle-class woman should spend most of her time at home fulfilling her many responsibilities. It is the wife's role to distribute wisely the property and goods her husband brings in through his efforts, position, or income. She should not be stingy or extravagant, keeping a check on the accounts to make sure that expenditures do not exceed income. She should see that her house is kept in good order by her servants. Even if she does not do her own cooking, she should know how to prepare food so that she can supervise the kitchen staff and see that all goes well when her husband brings guests home. Her children should be well cared for but not coddled by their nurse. Her husband should be served well and his peace protected when he returns home. His meals should be ready and she should greet him cheerfully, helping him to forget his worries. If he is in a bad temper, she should soothe him with soft words rather than respond with anger. She should not bother him with her own problems or argue with the servants at dinner.

The wise mistress of the household will get up early. After she attends Mass or says her prayers, she will give orders to the servants according to the needs of the day. Then she will take up some useful work herself, such as spinning or sewing. After her chambermaids have finished their tasks, she will expect them to spin or sew. She will buy flax at the market at a good price, have it spun by her own servants or by women of the town, and have it made into fine sheets and towels, which she will keep white and sweet smelling and maintain in chests. She will see that nothing is wasted in her household but will give leftover food and old clothes to the poor. Her charity will not be limited to giving away leftovers, but she will give wine and food from her own provisions to poor women in childbed, invalids, and poor neighbors.

She will be a model of hospitality and will delight in using her provisions and the fine possessions in her household to entertain guests, welcoming her husband's friends and associates and speaking courteously to everyone. To her neighbors she will be generous, lending them things when they have need of them and showing them friendship. To her servants she will be kind, reproving them gently when they misbehave.

The above instructions pertain to wealthy middle-class women who had many servants. Christine also provides instructions for artisans' wives, who belonged to the lower middle-class and had to do much more work themselves.[41] An artisan's wife should be diligent in taking care of her household and in helping her husband with his trade. She should urge her husband and his workmen to begin work early in the morning and to stop late at night, for one cannot make a good living in a trade without putting in many hours. Working along with her husband, she should learn the business well enough to direct the workmen herself. She should advise her husband not to undertake any work through which he may suffer a loss and to do as little work as possible on credit. She should treat her husband well and make their home comfortable so that he will not want to frequent the taverns, where many artisans are found. She herself should not gad about the town, gossiping with neighbors and visiting friends. She should encourage her husband to live prudently so that they will not run into debt. If she has children, she should first send them to school and later apprentice them to a trade so that they will be able to earn their own living.

Christine addresses a chapter of the *Livre des trois vertus* to the wives of country laborers.[42] She states that it is scarcely necessary to forbid them to wear expensive ornaments and extravagant clothes since they are well protected from all that by their poverty. Nor do they have to be admonished to be temperate in eating and drinking since they are commonly nourished with black bread, bacon, and soup, and their thirst is quenched with water. Nevertheless, although they have trials enough to bear, their lives are often more secure and more abundant than the lives of those who are seated in high places. Christine idealizes the "golden age" simplicity of the life of the poor peasant women. Idealization of the poor often was meant to suggest criticism of the rich. Since she could not have expected illiterate peasant women to read her book, this picture of the virtuous poor may have been meant to influence the rich to lead more useful, moral lives. It is also possible that she wanted to provide her aristocratic audience with a reassuring picture of the laboring poor.

Christine states that the wife of the country laborer should be hardworking and honest, and she should encourage her husband to be the same. If they are working the land for others, they should do it as well and as diligently as if they were doing it for themselves. At harvest time they should pay their master with wheat if that was grown on the land, not mixing in oats and pretending that nothing else was grown there. They should neither hide the best ewes and rams at the neighbors' farm when the master comes in order to pay him with inferior animals, nor pretend that their best animals are dead by showing him the skins of others, nor pay him with the worst fleeces. They should not give him a dishonest accounting of his carts or other property. The wife should give him an honest accounting of the poultry and eggs, of which she is in charge. They should not cut wood for building or firewood from the property of the master or another tenant without permission. When they look after the vineyards, they should perform the necessary tasks at the proper season. If they are commissioned by their master to hire seasonal workers, they should not pretend that they have paid seven groats a day if they have paid only four. In all such matters wives should urge their husbands to be honest.

Women should do what they can to help their husbands. They should not break down the hedges or allow their children to do it. They should not allow their children to steal grapes, fruit, or vegetables from anyone else's garden and should not steal anything themselves. They should prevent their animals from grazing in their neighbors' seeded fields or meadows. They should live in peace with their neighbors without going to court over trifles, as is the habit of many villagers. They should do unto their neighbors as they would have their neighbors do unto them, believe in God, go to church, and pay their tithes.

Christine even addresses a chapter of the *Livre des trois vertus* to prostitutes, women who were outside the pale of respectable society. She urges them to reform and give up their degrading way of life.

> How is it possible for a woman, who by her very nature and condition is honest, simple, and modest, to fall so low that she can endure such baseness, living, drinking, and eating among men who are worse than swine, or to be acquainted with only such people as these, who beat you, drag you about and threaten you, and because of whom you find yourself daily in danger of death? Alas, why is the simplicity and honesty of a woman brought to such wantonness in you? Ah, for Heaven's sake, you who bear the name of Christians and convert it to such baseness, get up and leave such dreadful mud and do not allow your poor soul to be burdened any longer with such filth committed by vile bodies, for God in His pity is prepared to receive you in his mercy if you wish to repent and cry for mercy in great contrition.[43]

She considers the reasons why a prostitute might be discouraged from reforming: the "dishonest people she frequents" would not allow it, respectable people would reject her, and she would not be able to support herself. Christine states that if the prostitute is determined to reform and shows her determination by dressing respectably, keeping away from old meeting places, and going to church frequently, her former associates will not bother her. If any man insists on pursuing her, she can get the protection of the law. Once people see that she has reformed and is leading a good, honest life, they will be glad to associate with her. She will be able to earn a living through honest work, "for if she has a body strong enough to do evil and to suffer bad nights, blows and numerous other misfortunes, she should be strong enough to earn her living.[44] People could take her in to help with the laundry in the great houses, she

111

could spin, care for women lying in, or nurse the sick. She would live in a little room on a respectable street among good people. She should live simply and soberly without getting drunk, should not be ill-tempered or quarrelsome, should not gossip, and should make sure that no unseemly or dishonest word comes from her mouth. She should always be courteous, humble, gentle, and full of good works to all people. She should make sure not to attract any men, or she would again ruin her reputation. In this way she could earn her living and profit more from one cent honestly earned than from a hundred received in sin. Christine's discussion is moralistic, but it is liberated for her time. Once again, it is unlikely that prostitutes would have read her book. Her aim probably was to influence people's attitudes toward prostitutes who were trying to reform, and to encourage them to help such women.

The neglect of women's economic roles in the courtesy books is surprising. The aristocratic audience for most of the books is a partial explanation, but we do not even find discussions of the role of aristocratic women in managing land and property. The statements made in *The Good Wife Taught Her Daughter* indicate that the mother and daughter made cloth for sale and possibly brewed ale; but rather than discussing these activities, the author simply tells the girl not to linger in town and to return home as soon as she has accomplished her business.[45]

There was a conflict between the ideal of behavior set forth for women and the jobs they had to perform in the real world, particularly for middle-class women. On the one hand, they were expected to be competent businesswomen and artisans. Merchants' wives had to handle their husbands' businesses while they were away, managing such transactions as buying and selling merchandise, paying bills, keeping accounts, dealing with customers, and stalling creditors. When their husbands were in town, they assisted them with their work. Artisans' wives learned their husbands' trades and were sufficiently skilled to train apprentices and run the shop by themselves, which required a great deal of assertiveness, independence, and responsibility.

On the other hand, the courtesy books admonish women to be humble, meek, and obedient. They are told to be sweet and gentle and to comply with all of their husbands' requests. Furthermore, they are exhorted to observe an ideal of retiring modesty in public.

When it comes to deportment, they are told to walk daintily, keep their eyes lowered, and keep their bodies still. When it comes to speech, they are told to keep their voices low, not to talk too much, and not to laugh, jest, or swear. This ideal of modesty would have been hard for women to follow when they were doing business in a man's world.

Rather than alter the ideal of feminine modesty or admit its impracticality under certain conditions, most of the authors of the courtesy books neglected women's roles in the outside world. Perhaps there was also a reluctance to acknowledge women's growing economic importance, or a failure to see it. It does not seem coincidental that the only author to portray women's economic roles fully within society was a woman. Rather than downplaying women's economic importance, Christine de Pizan publicized it and wished to give women an education that would better prepare them to meet their responsibilities.

VII

Ideals in the Courtesy Books as Related to the Lives of Medieval Women

In spite of the economic responsibility assumed by women of all social classes, they occupied a subservient position and possessed few legal rights. The feudal system curtailed the property rights of women and lowered their status.[1] Feudal practices are set forth in the *Tractate* ascribed to Richard Glanvill, an Anglo-Norman lawyer. It describes the laws and customs of England during the reign of Henry II (1154-89), but many of these practices were followed almost until modern times. When a woman married, her husband gave her a dower, which was the life use of one-third of his property at the time of their marriage without regard to later gains or losses. This proportion might not be increased even by agreement between husband and wife. The law regarding the dower was later made more generous. Under Henry III, a widow was permitted to receive one-third of the property her husband had owned at the time of his death. Under Edward IV, the law was revised to allow a husband to leave all of his property to his wife, but men rarely took advantage of this provision. The law of primogeniture discriminated against women in favor of male heirs. A man could not leave his main dwelling house to his wife since it belonged to his heir.

A woman had no control of her dower during the lifetime of her husband and could not interfere with his management of it. Parents gave a girl a dowry of property or money at her marriage. This also belonged to her husband as long as the marriage lasted, and he had a life interest in the dowry if she should die first. If her husband died first, a widow was entitled to the life use of her dower and dowry. Widows were the most independent women in medieval

society, both economically and legally. While her husband was
alive, a woman was bound by his will. According to Glanville, the
husband and wife were one person, and that person was the husband.

Before a girl was married, she was under her family's control.
Afterwards, that control passed to her husband. Unless she became
a widow, a woman was in a perpetual state of guardianship and had
little to say about her own destiny. This state of affairs existed at
every level of society. Noblewomen sometimes had less to say about
their destiny than women at lower social levels since their marriages
were determined by political considerations. When Eleanor of
Aquitaine was a mere girl of fifteen, she was married to Louis VII of
France, whose temperament differed drastically from hers, since it
seemed advisable to unite her extensive lands to the French crown.
She was fortunate enough to obtain a divorce and marry Henry II of
England, with whom she had more in common. Their two strong
personalities eventually clashed, however, and Eleanor left Henry
to establish her own court at Poitiers. Exasperated by her actions
and by the rebellions being fomented at her court, Henry came to
Poitiers in 1174 to sieze her and brought her back to England as his
prisoner. She was locked up in Salisbury Tower and remained a
prisoner, being kept there and in other strongly fortified places until
Henry's death in 1189.[2] One of the most powerful queens of the
Middle Ages thus spent fifteen years as a prisoner because she dared
to challenge her husband.

Families belonging to the gentry sought to place their daughters in the homes of powerful lords or rich patrons since they felt
their chances of making a good marriage would be increased. Iso-
lated from friends and family, the girls often experienced harsh
discipline, lack of affection, and loneliness. Nevertheless, their ambitious parents showed little concern about their feelings. Dorothy
Plumpton was placed in a household where she was lonely and
unhappy. She sent "diverse messages and writings" to her father
urging him to let her come home but received no reply. Finally, she
wrote, " it is thought in these parts...that you have little favour
unto me, the which errour you may now quench, if it will like you
to be so good and kind a father unto me."[3] Still she was not allowed
to come home. When Jane Stonor's daughter complained about
being unhappy in the household in which she was serving, Jane
reminded her that she had been placed there by Queen Elizabeth

Woodville, and told her that she could not be allowed to come home without the queen's permission.[4] Agnes Paston was even less sympathetic to her daughter Elizabeth. In response to her complaints about conditions in the household of Lady Pole, she wrote that "she must use hyrselfe to werke redyly as other jentylwomen don, and sumwhat to helpe hyrselfe therwyth."[5] Parents hoped that by remaining within these households, their daughters would attract the attention of young men of good social standing.

Marriages were arranged by families on the basis of economic considerations, and girls had little to say about the matter; however, since their consent had to be obtained to make the marriage valid, parents sometimes resorted to coercion. Agnes Paston tried to marry her twenty-year-old daughter Elizabeth to a wealthy but disfigured widower of fifty named Stephen Scrope. When Elizabeth protested, her mother beat her once or twice a week for several months so that her head was "broken in two or three places." Finally Elizabeth consented; but fortunately for her, the marriage did not go through. Her sister-in-law reported that her mother was impatient to be "delivered of her," and several other plans for her marriage were made, but none of them materialized. She eventually married Robert Poynings, second son of Robert, fourth Lord Poynings, and had a son who later became Sir Edward.[6] After a great deal of bullying by her mother, she thus wound up with a husband who satisfied the ambitions of her family.

Occasionally, girls were bold enough to try to select their own husbands, but they faced ostracism and a great deal of criticism, particularly if they chose a man below their rank. This was the case with Margery Paston, Agnes's granddaughter and the daughter of John and Margaret Paston. She fell in love with a young man named Richard Calle, the chief bailiff of the Paston estate, and betrothed herself to him. When she informed her mother of the situation, Margaret was furious (her father was already dead at the time). She got the Bishop of Norwich to examine Margery to find out if she had formally pledged herself. Margery boldly asserted that if the words she used had not made her betrothal sure, she would make it surer before she departed.[7] Margery returned to her home to find its doors closed to her by her mother's order. Margery and Richard stayed at a convent in Blackborough until her family's opposition relented enough to permit their marriage. Margery's brothers disapproved of the match as strongly as her mother. John Paston III contemptuously wrote that Richard Calle "shold never have my good wyll for to make my sustyr to selle kandyll and mustard in Framlyngham."[8] Although Margaret relented enough to leave a legacy to Margery's oldest son, Margery's family never forgave her for marrying below her rank.

Middle-class girls had just as little say in choosing their husbands as gentlewomen. Marriage was a perfectly respectable way of obtaining capital, and merchants often shopped around for a good dowry in selecting a wife. The young merchant made businesslike inquiries and was ready to pay a commission on the dowry to a broker. John Lyonhill, goldsmith, agreed to pay a clerk ten pounds out of a dowry of eighty pounds for arranging his marriage with the daughter of a senior member of his company. Another goldsmith married on a promise of forty pounds. William Nightingale, draper, married on the promise of one hundred pounds, a gold ring, a gray fur, a horse described as "an Irish heavy," and a thirty-four-year lease of a quay. Thomas Bataill, mercer, being offered forty marks to marry a niece of Sir William Plumpton, insisted that his future wife's family should board them both for three years and lend him one hundred marks during that period for his business.[9] An artisan might well be interested in finding a widow who had been married to a man in his trade so that he could take over the shop. Guild regulations recognized and encouraged such arrangements. With such deals being common, a middle-class woman would not have felt that she was being selected for her charms.

In the case of peasants, particularly serfs, both men and women were subservient to their overlord and were not free in regard to marriage. They had to pay a fine called the *merchet* for getting married. This was always paid by serfs and was sometimes paid by freemen as an incident of their land tenure. No marriage between serfs could take place without the lord's consent, which usually involved another fine. A fine was always involved if a woman married into another manor, thus depriving her lord of her prospective brood. When serfs from two different manors married, the lords sometimes indemnified themselves by sharing the children produced by the marriage. It was profitable for lords when their serfs married and had children. Therefore, they sometimes asserted a right to force serfs to marry. On the manors of Saint Albans in the opening years of the fourteenth century, fines were paid to remain without a mate for a year or for life, or for disobedience in refusing to take a particular mate. Lords tried to force widows to marry since they wanted to have a strong male arm to work the farm to the fullest extent, and to insure payment of all manorial obligations. At Brightwaltham, six widows who had come into holdings and could not render the labor that was due were ordered to provide themselves with husbands.[10]

Some fines were particularly demeaning to women. On certain manors, custom demanded a fine from newly married peasant couples as an alternative to the *jus primae noctis*, the lord's right of passing the first night with the bride.[11] The serf had the power of redemption, and the lord was more interested in collecting fines than in deflowering peasant girls, but the custom was still insulting to women even though it was exacted in the form of a money payment. A bondwoman had to pay a fine of *leyrwite* for incontinency. Since she was considered the lord's chattel, any deterioration of her value had to be made good. A violation of her chastity was a violation of his property. If the offender herself could not pay, then the nearest male relative had to pay as the person responsible for the woman.[12]

According to the social ideal for women of all classes, from the aristocracy to the peasantry, the good woman was submissive and the bad woman disobedient. The subservience of women was considered the natural state of things rather than a mere social reality. The disorderly, dominant woman was a symbol of chaos.[13] In the mystery plays, Noah's disobedient wife represents the corruption of the world before the flood. Popular festivals in which men dressed as women were occasions for carnivalesque disorder in pre-industrial Europe. The dominant role of Nicolette in *Aucassin and Nicolette* is part of a topsy-turvy world in which kings lie in childbed and queens fight wars—not by killing people, but by throwing huge cheeses into a river and seeing who can make the biggest splash. If wars must be fought, throwing cheeses might be better than shooting cannons. The author subtly criticizes the brutality of war by presenting this comic alternative. The theme of the dominant woman, the woman on top, sometimes went along with criticism of the established order. When this occurred, the unruly woman was a speaker of the truth. Erasmus's Dame Folly is a famous example of this type.[14] Most of the time, however, the unruly woman was a negative symbol.

The ideals set forth in the courtesy books reflect the subordination that existed in life. Regardless of her rank, every woman is told to be humble, modest, and obedient. As an unmarried girl, she is told to obey her parents and follow their wishes. Most of her training is directed at making her a docile wife. As a married woman, she is told to love and obey her husband. Although girls did not choose their husbands, it was assumed that love between a married couple would grow. If it did not, the wife was still obliged to obey her husband. Medieval marriage was a business proposition, and although love and marriage were not considered incompatible, obedience was more important than romance.

The works of the Church Fathers provided a foundation that led to a very restrictive theory regarding women's place in society. The Church Fathers were addressing mainly virgins and widows, but their ideas were applied to wives and women who intended to marry. The ideal of virginity was exalted for young girls, who were exhorted to preserve their sexual purity and modesty before marriage. In the case of wives, the ideal of virginity was converted to that of chastity, which was considered the foundation for a woman's honor. The same virtues of humility, obedience, modesty, piety, and chastity are prescribed for virgins, widows, and wives. This moral code went along with an asceticism that frowned upon the wearing of makeup, tinting hair, using artificial means to enhance beauty, wearing revealing clothes, eating rich food, drinking wine, and indulging in luxury. This standard of behavior was most convenient for upper-class husbands who were concerned about preserving the purity of their line and the fullness of their treasury. It was in the interest of the Church and the aristocracy to maintain the subjection of women. The Church subordinated woman to her husband, while feudalism subordinated her to her fief or overlord.[15]

The ideal of the coquette and the doctrine of courtly love had some influence in improving the image of women. After centuries of clerical antifeminism, it must have been refreshing for women to have their beauty praised as an inspiration to men rather than condemned as their downfall. This ideal gave women a certain amount of freedom, particularly at the courts of Provence during the twelfth century. Nevertheless, in most places and at most times during the Middle Ages, the freedom was an illusion. For instance, when Philip the Fair's daughters-in-law, Marguerite and Blanche of Burgundy, gave purses of cloth of gold to two young knights and were suspected of adultery, the young men were flayed alive, and the women were thrown into prison in Château-Gaillard. Marguerite admitted her misconduct and soon perished in the dungeon, while Blanche protested her innocence and was sent to a convent for the rest of her life.[16] The ideal of the coquette was a vehicle for fantasy and a safety valve for forbidden feelings. If any woman committed adultery and was caught, she was punished severely.

The emphasis on the sexual and familial roles of women in the courtesy books written by men seems to indicate an anxiety about women overreaching their domain. This is corroborated by the lack of attention given to the political and economic roles of women. In spite of the importance of the queen in the early Middle Ages and the existence of powerful figures like Eleanor of Aquitaine and Blanche of Castille in the later period, a mirror for the princess does not appear until the late thirteenth century. The only mirror for the princess that portrays fully the queen's political responsibilities is Christine de Pizan's *Livre des trois vertus*. Works dealing with the economic roles of women are just as scarce. The only treatises that suggest the wide range of occupations practiced by women during the Middle Ages are Francesco Barberino's *Reggimento e costumi di donna* and Christine de Pizan's *Livre des trois vertus*. Although Barberino addresses women of all social classes, he focuses upon their familial roles. Only Christine provides an accurate picture of the full range of women's responsibilities within the familial, social, political, and economic spheres. She wished to have society acknowledge the importance of women and give them an education that would help them meet those responsibilities.

The voice of one feminist could do little to combat the ideal for women that was developed in most of the courtesy books. It was an ideal of passivity and claustration. Although medieval women needed to exercise the active virtues in leading their lives, the passive ones were emphasized in the courtesy books. Femininity was equated with modesty, humility, chastity, and obedience. Women were exhorted to see themselves in the mirror of men's eyes and to act as servant, nurse, lover, wife, and mother to meet the needs of men. Although women played important roles in the political and economic spheres, their duties within the home were emphasized, and the household was considered their proper domain.

This ideal continued through centuries to come and became a useful tool for the indoctrination of women. In later periods, it was closer to the reality of women's lives. From the sixteenth to the eighteenth century, the subjugation of women gradually increased.[17] The patriarchal family streamlined itself for more efficient property acquisition, social mobility, and preservation of the line. The extension of commercial capitalism bureaucratized and institutionalized society. Work was moved out of the home and into the factory, while women were kept within the home. The feminine ideal of behavior, as developed in the courtesy books, suited this social pattern because it defined women's place as the home. By the eighteenth century, married women in France and England had even less legal right to make decisions on their own about dowries and possessions than during the Middle Ages. Women in prosperous families did not engage in productive labor since working was not considered "ladylike." Those in poor families were given the most ill-paid menial positions. With the exception of menial workers, women were restricted more and more to the private realm. In 1868, F. J. Furnivall, an editor of *The Good Wife Taught Her Daughter*, stated that the poem "bears trace of the greater freedom of action allowed to women in early times."[18] The Victorian "doll's house" was more of a prison for women than the medieval castle. Women had to wait for the feminism and industrialism of the nineteenth and twentieth centuries to begin to release them from their tower.

Notes

CHAPTER I

1. Geoffrey Chaucer, *The Works of Geoffrey Chaucer*, ed. F. N. Robinson (Boston: Houghton Mifflin, 1957), p. 39.

2. Joan Ferrante, *Woman as Image in Medieval Literature* (New York: Columbia University Press, 1975), pp. 65-67.

3. Ibid., p. 37.

4. Ibid., p. 43.

5. Guillaume de Lorris and Jean de Meun, *The Romance of the Rose*, trans. Charles Dahlberg (Princeton: Princeton University Press, 1971), pp. 32-41.

6. Ibid., pp. 222-225.

7. Chaucer, p. 21.

8. For a discussion of the evolution of the ideal of the knight, see Diane Bornstein, *Mirrors of Courtesy* (Hamden, Connecticut: Archon Books, 1975).

CHAPTER II

1. George Tavard, *Woman in Christian Tradition* (Notre Dame: University of Notre Dame Press, 1973), p. 59.

2. Ibid., pp. 61-62.

3. Ibid., pp. 102-103.

4. Ibid., p. 107.

5. Ambrose, "De virginibus ad Marcellinam sororem suam," in *Patrologiae cursus completus*, ed. J. P. Migne (Paris, 1845), XVI, 187-234.

6. Alice A. Hentsch, *De la littérature didactique du moyen âge s'adressant spécialement aux femmes* (Halle: Université de Halle-Wittenberg, 1903), p. 22.

7. Ambrose, "*Ad virginem devotam,*" in *Patrologiae cursus completus*, XVII, 579-84.

8. F. A. Wright, ed., *Select Letters of Jerome* (Cambridge, Mass.: Harvard University Press, 1963), pp. 483-93.

9. Ibid., p. 57.

10. Ibid., pp. 345-47.

11. Ibid., pp. 95, 103.

12. Tavard, *Woman in Christian Tradition*, pp. 113-18.

13. Frances and Joseph Gies, *Women in the Middle Ages* (New York: Barnes & Noble, 1980), p. 65.

14. Saint Caesarius, *Patrologiae cursus completus*, LXVII, 1103-21, 1128-35.

15. Ibid., 1135-38.

16. Aldhelm, *Patrologiae cursus completus*, LXXXIX, 103-62.

17. Ibid., 237-80.

18. Oswald Cockayne, ed., *Hali Meidenhad* (London: EETS, OS, 18, 1866).

19. that ilke unhende flesches brune. that bearninde yecthe of that licomliche lust. bifore that wlatefulle werc. that schomelese somnunge. that fulthe of fulthe stinkende. & untohe dede. Ibid., p. 9. The translation is my own.

20. Ibid., pp. 30-31. This translation and the ones that follow are those of the editor.

21. Ibid., pp. 34-35.

22. Ibid., pp. 37-38.

23. M. B. Salu, trans., *The Ancrene Riwle* (Notre Dame: University of Notre Dame Press, 1955). This translation is based on the manuscript edited by Mabel Day, *The English Text of the Ancrene Riwle, Edited from Cotton Ms. Nero A XIV* (London: EETS, OS, 225, 1952).

24. Salu, *The Ancrene Riwle*, p. 102.

25. Maureen Slattery Durley, "The Crowned Dame, Dame Opinion, and Dame Philosophy: The Female Characteristics of Three Ideals in Christine de Pizan's *Lavision Christine*," in *Ideals for Women in the Works of Christine de Pizan*, ed. Diane Bornstein (Ann Arbor: Medieval Monographs, 1981), pp. 29-50.

26. For a modern edition, see Maureen Curnow, ed., "The *Livre de la Cité des dames*: A Critical Edition" (Vanderbilt University Dissertation, 1975).

27. Christine Reno, "Virginity as an Ideal in Christine de Pizan's *Cité des dames*," in *Ideals for Women in the Works of Christine de Pizan*, pp. 69-90.

28. Katherine M. Rogers, *The Troublesome Helpmate: a History of Misogyny in Literature* (Seattle: University of Washington Press, 1966), pp. 14-22.

29. Georges Duby, *Medieval Marriage*, trans. Elborg Forster (Baltimore: Johns Hopkins University Press, 1978), p. 7.

CHAPTER III

1. Georges Duby, *Medieval Marriage*, trans. Elborg Forster (Baltimore: Johns Hopkins University Press, 1978), pp. 10-14.

Notes

2. Ibid., pp. 102-3.

3. Ibid., p. 14.

4. Garin lo Brun, "L'Enseignement de Garin lo Brun," ed. Carl Appel, *Revue des Langues Romanes*, 33 (1889), 409-29.

5. Matfre Ermengaud, *Le Breviari d'Amor de Matfre Ermengaud*, ed. Peter T. Ricketts (Leiden: J. Brill, 1976), p. 165.

6. Ibid., pp. 155-90.

7. Giuseppe Palazzi, ed., *Le Poesie Inedite di Sordello* (Venice: Tipografia Antonelli, 1887), pp. 21-59.

8. Joan Ferrante, *Woman as Image in Medieval Literature* (New York: Columbia University Press, 1975), p. 123.

9. Karl Bartsch, ed., *Provenzalisches Lesebuch* (Elberfeld: R. L. Friderichs, 1855), pp. 140-48.

10. L. Constans, ed., "La Cour d'Amour," *Revue des Langues Romanes*, ser. 3, VI (1881), 157-79, 209-20, 261-76.

11. Gustav Körting, ed., *L'Art d'amors und Li Remedes d'amor: zwei altfranzösische Lehrgedicte von Jacques d'Amiens* (Leipzig: F. C. W. Vogel, 1868), pp. 50-68.

12. Auguste Doutrepont, ed., *La Clef d'amors* (Halle: Max Niemeyer, 1890), pp. 79-126.

13. Meg Bogin, *The Women Troubadours* (New York: Paddington Press, 1976), pp. 50-51.

14. Ibid., pp. 63-64.

15. Ibid., p. 68.

16. Ibid., p. 81.

17. Ibid., p. 89.

18. Ibid., p. 113.

19. John J. Parry, trans., *The Art of Courtly Love* (New York: Norton, 1969), p. 13.

20. Amy Kelly, *Eleanor of Aquitaine and the Four Kings* (Cambridge, Mass.: Harvard University Press, 1951), p. 99.

21. John F. Benton, "The Court of Champagne as a Literary Center," *Speculum*, 36 (1961), 551-91.

22. Ibid., p. 589.

23. June Hall Martin McCash, "Marie de Champagne and Eleanor of Aquitaine: a Relationship Re-examined," *Speculum*, 54 (1979), 698-711.

24. Benton, p. 587.

25. Chrétien de Troyes, *Le Chevalier de la Charrete*, ed. Mario Roques (Paris: Champion, 1972), pp. 1-2.

26. Parry, *The Art of Courtly Love*, pp. 167-77.

27. Christine de Pizan, *Le Trésor de la Cité des dames selon dame Cristine* (Paris: Anthoine Verard, 1497), sig. f iii-v.

CHAPTER IV

1. Georges Duby, *Medieval Marriage*, trans. E. Forster (Baltimore: Johns Hopkins University Press, 1978), p. 15.

2. Ibid., pp. 4-5.

3. Alice A. Hentsch, *De la littérature didactique du moyen âge s'adressant spécialement aux femmes* (Halle: Université de Halle Wittenberg, 1903), p. 75.

4. The original letter does not survive. A copy of it is recorded in *La Vie de Saint Louis par le Confesseur de la Reine Marguerite*, edited by Daunou and Naudet, *Recueil des historiens des Gaules et de la France* (Paris: Imprimerie Royale, 1840), XX, 82-83.

5. Fille, quant venez à la table pour mangier, vous ne devez mie querre seulement le delect de la bouche, mais vostre soustenance, et penser à Dieu tant que vous ne prenez plus que vous ne devez. Saint Louis, "Conseils de Saint Louis à une de ses Filles," in *Recueil des historiens des Gaules et de la France*, eds. De Wailly, Delisle, Jourdain (Paris: Imprimerie Royale, 1840), XXIII, 132. The translation is my own.

6. Fille, se vous voulez parler à homme, mectez garde que vous ne dictes chose ou l'on puisse mal penser; mais dictes parolles qui touchent à bon ediffiement, par quoy on puist jugier que vous estes fille saige et bien advisée. Ibid., p. 133.

7. William Caxton, *The Book of the Knight of the Tower*, ed. M. Y. Offord (London: EETS, SS, 2, 1971), pp. xviii-xix.

8. Ibid., p. 35.

9. Ibid., p. 36.

10. Ibid., p. 37.

11. Ibid., p. 133.

12. Hentsch, *Littérature didactique*, pp. 172-75.

13. Hermann Knust, ed., "Castigos y dotrinas que un sabio dava a sus hijas," in *Dos obras didacticas y dos legendas sacadas de manuscritos de la Biblioteca del Escorial* (Madrid, 1878), p. 269.

14. Ibid., p. 292.

15. Jerome Pichon, ed., *Le Ménagier de Paris* (Paris: Crapelet, 1846), I, 22-28.

16. Ibid., I, 91.

17. Ibid., I, 125.

18. Ibid., I, 168-69. Translation by Eileen Power, *The Goodman of Paris* (New York: Harcourt, 1928), pp. 171-72.

19. Pichon, *Le Ménagier de Paris*, I, 32.

20. Robert of Blois, *Robert von Blois sämtliche Werke*, ed. Jacob Ulrich (Berlin: Mayer & Muller, 1889), p. 61.

21. Gardez que nus home sa main
    Ne laissiez matre en votre sain,
    Fors celui qui le droit i a.

Sachiez, qui premiers controva
Affiche, que por ce le fist,
Que nues hons sa main ne meist
En soin de fome, ou il n'ait droit,
Que espousee ne li soit.
Cil l'i puet matre sanz forfait,
Qui dou sorplus son plaisir fait.
Quant qu'il voudra, bien le sosfrez
Qu'obedience li davez,
Con li moinnes fait a l'abé.

Ibid., pp. 59-60. The translation is my own.

22. William M. Rossetti, "Italian Courtesy Books," in *A Booke of Precedence*, ed. F. J. Furnivall (London: EETS, ES, 8, 1869), pp. 36-38. Hentsch, *Littérature didactique*, p. 104.

23. Francesco Barberino, *Del reggimento e costumi di donna*, in *Collezione di opere inedite o rare dei primi tre secoli della lingua*, ed. Carlo Baudi di Vesme (Bologna: Presso Gaetano Romagnoli, 1875), II, 118-201.

24. Eugene Oswald, "Early German Courtesy Books," in *A Booke of Precedence*, p. 140.

25. Hentsch, *Littérature didactique*, p. 48.

26. *Die Winsbekin*, in *König Tirol, Winsbeke und Winsbekin*, ed. Albert Leitzmann (Halle: Max Niemeyer, 1888), pp. 47-60.

27. W. T. H. Jackson, "Faith Unfaithful—The German Reaction to Courtly Love," in *The Meaning of Courtly Love*, ed. F. X. Newman (Albany: State University of New York Press, 1968), pp. 55-76.

28. Pietro Gori, ed., *Dodici avvertimenti che deve dare la madre alla figliuola quando la manda a marito* (Florence: A. Salani, 1885).

29. Tauno F. Mustanoja, ed., *The Good Wife Taught Her Daughter. The Good Wyfe Wold a Pylgremage. The Thewis of Gud Women* (Helsinki, 1948), p. 126.

30. Ibid., p. 172.

31. Ibid., p. 163.

32. Ibid., p. 161.

33. Ibid., p. 174.

34. Ibid., pp. 173-74.

35. Ibid., pp. 176-96.

36. Christine de Pizan, *The Book of Three Virtues*, trans. Charity C. Willard (unpublished translation, 1975), pp. 41-42. There is no modern edition of the French text. An early printed edition is *Le Trésor de la Cité des dames selon dame Cristine* (Paris: Anthoine Verard, 1497).

37. Ibid., p. 47.

38. Christine de Pizan, *The Boke of the Cyte of Ladyes*, in *Distaves and*

Dames, ed. Diane Bornstein (Delmar, N. Y.: Scholars' Facsimiles & Reprints, 1978), sig. KK v.

39. Hentsch, *Littérature didactique*, p. 199.

40. A. M. Chazaud, ed., *Les Enseignements d'Anne de France à sa fille Suzanne de Bourbon* (Moulins: C. Desrosiers, 1878), p. xxxi. Christine de Pizan evidently was one of Anne's favorite authors. She owned three large anthologies of her works. Five volumes of Christine's works were bound in red velvet and placed together on a bookshelf. See Chazaud's inventory of Anne's library, pp. 255-56.

41. Or pensez donc, ma fille, puisque ainsi est, que vous qui estes feminine et foible créature, devez donc bien mectre peine, quelque heureuse fortune que puissez jamais avoir, à vous conduire gracieusement, en parfaicte humilité, par espécial, envers vostre seigneur et mary, auquel, après Dieu, vous devez parfaicte amour et obéissance, et ne vous y povez trop fort humilier, ne trop porter d'honneur, et le devez servir en toutes ses necessitéz, et luy estre doulce, privée et amyable, et aussi à tous ses parens et amys, à chascun selon son degré. Ibid., pp. 47-48. The translation is my own.

42. Pour quelconque estrange ou mal plaisant alliance ou vous puissez estre, ne vous en mérencoliez ne desconfortez ains devez louer Dieu, et croire qu'il est tout juste, et que jamais ne fait rien qui ne soit raisonnable. Donc, ma fille, s'il advenoit que y fussiez fortunée, et que y eussiez beaucoup à souffrir, aiez parfaicte pascience, en vous actendant du tout à la voulenté et bon plaisir du Créateur. Ibid., pp. 72-73.

43. Diane Bornstein, "Women's Public and Private Space in Some Medieval Courtesy Books," *Centerpoint*, 3 (1980), 68-74.

CHAPTER V

1. Marion F. Facinger, "A Study of Medieval Queenship: Capetian France, 987-1237," *Studies in Medieval and Renaissance History*, 5 (1968), 1-27.

2. Ibid., pp. 28-31.

3. Ibid., pp. 32-37.

4. Lester K. Born, trans., *The Education of a Christian Prince by Desidirius Erasmus* (New York: Columbia University Press, 1936), pp. 99-124.

5. Robert Fawtier, *The Capetian Kings of France*, trans. Lionel Butler and R. J. Adam (London: Macmillan, 1960), pp. 127-30.

6. Joseph Strayer, *The Reign of Philip the Fair* (Princeton: Princeton University Press, 1980), p. 9.

7. Ibid., pp. 14-18.

8. F. Funck-Brentano, *The Middle Ages*, trans. Elizabeth O'Neill (London: William Heinemann, 1922), p. 417.

9. Strayer, *The Reign of Philip the Fair*. p. 67.

10. Fawtier, *The Capetian Kings of France*, p. 4.

11. Born, *The Education of a Christian Prince*, p. 118.

12. Alice Hentsch, *La Littérature didactique du moyen âge s'adressant spécialement aux femmes* (Halle: Université de Halle-Wittenberg, 1903), pp. 99-104.

13. Durand de Champagne, *Le Miroir des dames*, Bibliothèque Nationale, f. fr. 610, fols. 9v, 36. Neither the Latin version nor the French has been edited.

14. Chastete est la tresgrant honneur des femmes et des dames, la tresgrant et vertueuse beaulte des ames et la tres souef flamant odeur de bonne renomee de la quelle parle le saige en Ecclesiastique. Ibid, fol. 88v. The translation is my own.

15. Ibid., fol. 104v.

16. Ibid., fol. 1v.

17. Christine de Pizan, *The Book of the Three Virtues*, trans. Charity C. Willard (unpublished translation, 1975), p. 15.

18. Suzanne Solente, ed., *Le Livre des fais et bonnes meurs du sage roy Charles V par Christine de Pisan*, I (Paris: SATF, 1936), 53-57.

19. Christine de Pizan, *The Book of the Three Virtues*, pp. 37-38.

20. *The Epistles on the Romance of the Rose and Other Documents in the Debate*, ed. Charles F. Ward (Chicago: University of Chicago, 1901).

21. Mathilde Laigle, *Le Livre des trois vertus de Christine de Pisan et son milieu historique et littéraire* (Paris: Champion, 1912), p. 8.

22. Christine de Pizan, "*The Boke of the Cyte of Ladyes*," trans. B. Anslay, in *Distaves and Dames*, ed. Diane Bornstein (Delmar, N. Y.: Scholars' Facsimiles and Reprints, 1978), sig. ff 1.

23. Ibid., sigs. ff 1-1v.

24. Ibid., sigs. cc 1-1v.

25. Ibid., sig. gg 11.

26. Christine Reno, "Virginity as an Ideal in Christine de Pizan's *Cité des dames*," in *Ideals for Women in the Works of Christine de Pizan*, ed. Diane Bornstein (Ann Arbor, Michigan: Medieval Monographs, 1981), pp. 69-90.

27. Christine de Pizan, *Cyte of Ladyes*, sig. hh vi.

28. Ibid., sig. hh vi-v.

29. Ibid., sig. II 1.

30. Frances and Joseph Gies, *Women in the Middle Ages* (New York: Barnes & Noble, 1980), p. 22.

31. Christine de Pizan, *Cyte of Ladyes*, sig. ff ii-v-iii.

32. Ibid., sig. II iii-v - iv-v. William Caxton, trans., *The Book of Faytes of Armes and of Chyvalrye*, ed. A. T. P. Byles (London: EETS, OS, 189, 1932), p. 108.

33. Christine de Pizan, *Cyte of Ladies*, sig. ff iii - iii-v. Blanche's virtues are again praised in Book II, Chapter 64, sig. Q ii.

34. Marcel Brion, *Blanche de Castille: femme de Louis VIII, mère de Saint Louis, 1188-1252* (Paris: Les Editions de France, 1939).

35. Christine de Pizan, *Cyte of Ladyes*, sig. ff iii-v.

36. Ibid., sig. ff iv.

37. Ibid., sig. Z iii.

CHAPTER VI

1. Margaret Wade Labarge, *A Baronial Household of the Thirteenth Century* (New York: Barnes & Noble, 1965), p. 55.

2. Ibid., p. 57.

3. H. S. Bennett, *The Pastons and their England* (Cambridge: Cambridge University Press, 1970), p. 68.

4. Norman Davis, ed., *Paston Letters and Papers of the Fifteenth Century* (Oxford: Oxford University Press, 1971). C. L. Kingsford, ed., *The Stonor Letters and Papers, 1290-1483* (London: Royal Historical Society, 1919).

5. David Herlihy, "Land, Family, and Women in Continental Europe, 701-1200," in *Women in Medieval Society*, ed. Susan M. Stuard (Philadelphia: University of Pennsylvania Press, 1976), pp. 13-45.

6. A. Abram, "Women Traders in Medieval London," *Economic Journal*, 26 (1916), p. 277.

7. Sylvia L. Thrupp, *The Merchant Class of Medieval London* (Ann Arbor: University of Michigan, 1948), p. 170.

8. Margery Kempe, *The Book of Margery Kempe*, eds. Sanford B. Meech, Hope Emily Allen (London: EETS, OS, 212, 1940), pp. 9-10.

9. Ibid., p. 10.

10. Ibid., p. 9.

11. Ibid., p. 9.

12. Thrupp, *The Merchant Class of Medieval London*, p. 18.

13. André Lehmann, *Le Rôle de la femme dans l'histoire de France au moyen âge* (Paris: Berger-Levrault, 1952), p. 437.

14. Ibid., pp. 436-37.

15. Abram, "Women Traders in Medieval London," p. 276.

16. Ibid., p. 277.

17. Lehmann, *Rôle de la femme dans l'histoire de France*, pp. 471-72.

18. Ibid., pp. 467-68.

19. Etienne Boileau, *Le Livre des métiers d'Etienne Boileau*, eds. R. de Lespinasse, F. Bonnardot (Paris: Imprimerie Nationale, 1879), p. cxx.

20. Ibid., pp. 70-71.

21. Ibid., p. 74.

22. Abram, "Women Traders in Medieval London," p. 278.

23. Boileau, *Livre des métiers*, p. lxxvi.

24. Lehmann, *Rôle de la femme dans l'histoire de France*, p. 417.

Notes

25. Christine de Pizan, "*The Boke of the Cyte of Ladyes*," in *Distaves and Dames*, ed. Diane Bornstein (Delmar, N. Y.: Scholars' Facsimiles and Reprints, 1978), sig. OO i-v.

26. Abram, "Women Traders in Medieval London," p. 277.

27. Lehmann, *Rôle de la femme dans l'histoire de France*, p. 417.

28. Abram, "Women Traders in Medieval London," p. 278.

29. Ibid., p. 281.

30. Rodney Hilton, *Bond Men Made Free* (New York: Viking Press, 1973), pp. 36-37.

31. Eileen Power, *Medieval Women* (Cambridge: Cambridge University Press, 1975), p. 71.

32. Lehmann, *Rôle de la femme dans l'histoire de France*, p. 196.

33. Francesco Barberino, *Del reggimento e costumi di donna*, ed. Carlo Baudi di Vesme, in *Collezione di opere inedite o rare dei primi tre secoli della lingua*, vol. II (Bologna: Presso Gaetano Romagnoli, 1875), pp. 297-300.

34. Ibid., pp. 301-3.

35. Ibid., pp. 305-24.

36. Ibid., pp. 325-29.

37. Ibid., pp. 331-36.

38. Christine de Pizan, *The Book of the Three Virtues*, trans. Charity C. Willard (unpublished translation, 1975), pp. 116-24.

39. Ibid., pp. 149-52.

40. Ibid., pp. 150-51.

41. Ibid., pp. 170-72.

42. Ibid., pp. 182-84.

43. Ibid., p. 177.

44. Ibid., p. 179.

45. Tauno F. Mustanoja, ed., *The Good Wife Taught Her Daughter. The Good Wyfe Wold a Pylgremage. The Thewis of Gud Women* (Helsinki, 1948), pp. 160-62.

CHAPTER VII

1. Willystine Goodsell, *A History of Marriage and the Family* (New York: Macmillan, 1935), pp. 225-27.

2. Amy Kelly, *Eleanor of Aquitaine and the Four Kings* (Cambridge, Mass.: Harvard University Press, 1951), pp. 183-202.

3. T. Stapleton, ed., *The Plumpton Correspondence* (London: Camden Society, 1839), p. 202.

4. C. L. Kingsford, ed., *The Stonor Letters* (London: Royal Historical Society, 1919), I, 122-23.

5. Norman Davis, ed., *Paston Letters and Papers of the Fifteenth Century* (Oxford: Oxford University Press, 1971), I, 42.

6. Ibid., p. lvi.

7. Ibid., p. 342.

8. Ibid., p. 541.

9. Sylvia Thrupp, *The Merchant Class of Medieval London* (Ann Arbor: University of Michigan, 1948), pp. 105-6.

10. G. G. Coulton, *The Medieval Village* (Cambridge: Cambridge University Press, 1931), p. 83.

11. Ibid., pp. 464-65.

12. Ibid., p. 81.

13. Natalie Z. Davis, "Women on Top," in *Society and Culture in Early Modern France* (Stanford: Stanford University Press, 1975), pp. 124-51.

14. Desidirius Erasmus, *The Praise of Folly*, trans. H. Hudson (Princeton: Princeton University Press [1941]).

15. Eileen Power, *Medieval Women* (Cambridge: Cambridge University Press, 1975), p. 19.

16. F. Funck-Brentano, *The Middle Ages* (London: William Heinemann, 1922), pp. 417-18.

17. Sibylle Harksen, *Women in the Middle Ages*, trans. M. Herzfeld (New York: Abner Schram, 1975), pp. 23, 28.

18. F. J. Furnivall, ed., *The Babees' Book* (London: EETS, OS, 32, 1868; reprinted New York: Greenwood Press, 1969), p. lxix.

Appendix

A Chronological List of Treatises by the Church Fathers and Medieval Courtesy Books for Women

2ND CENTURY	Tertullian, *Ad uxorem*
	De cultu feminarum
	De monogamia
3RD CENTURY	Cyprian, *De habitu virginum*
4TH CENTURY	Athanasius, *Exhortatio ad sponsam Christi*
	Ambrose, *Ad virginem devotam exhortatio*
	De institutione virginis
	De virginibus ad Marcellinam sororem suam
	De viduis
	Jerome, *Epistola ad Eustochium de custodia virginitatis* (383)
	Ad Laetam de institutione filiae (398)
5TH CENTURY	*Ad Theodoram viduam*
	Ad Salvinam (400, 405)
	Ad Hedibiam (406)
	Ad Ageruchiam de monogamia (409)
	Ad Demetriadem de servanda virginitate (414)
	Epistola ad Gaudentium de Pacatulae infantulae educatione (415)
	Avit, *De consolatoria laude castitatis ad Fuscinam sororem*
6TH CENTURY	Caesarius, *Regula ad virgines* (513)
	Ad Caesariam abbatissam ejusque congregationem
	Epistola hortatoria ad virginem Deo dedicatam
7TH CENTURY	Aldhelm, *De laudibus virginitatis sive de virginate sanctorum*
	De Laudibus virginum

133

12TH CENTURY	Etienne de Fougères, *Le Livre des manières*
	Garin lo Brun, *Ensenhamen*
13TH CENTURY	*The Ancrene Riwle*
	Hali Meidenhad
	Sordello, *Ensenhamens d'onor*
	La Cour d'amour
	Jacques d'Amiens, *L'Art d'amors*
	La Clef d'amors
	Matfre Ermengaud, *Le Breviari d'amor*
	Amanieu de Sescas, *Ensenhamen de la donzela*
	Die Winsbekin
	Robert de Blois, *Chastoiement des dames*
	Saint Louis, *Enseignements à sa fille Isabelle*
	Conseils de Saint Louis à une de ses filles
	Durand de Champagne, *Speculum dominarum*; translated as the *Miroir des dames* (before 1305)
14TH CENTURY	Francesco Barberino, *Del Reggimento e costumi di donna* (ca. 1307-15)
	Dodici avvertimenti
	Geoffrey de la Tour-Landry, *Le Livre du chevalier de la Tour-Landry* (ca. 1371-72)
	Le Ménagier de Paris (ca. 1392-94)
	The Good Wife Taught Her Daughter
15TH CENTURY	*The Good Wyfe Wold a Pylgremage*
	The Thewis of Gud Women
	Castigos y dotrinas que un sabio dava a sus hijas
	Christine de Pizan, *Le Livre des trois vertus* (ca. 1405)
	Le Livre de la Cité des dames (ca. 1405)
16TH CENTURY	Anne de Beaujeu, *Les Enseignements d'Anne de France à sa fille Suzanne de Bourbon* (ca. 1504-5)

Bibliography

PRIMARY SOURCES

Alberti, Leon Battista. *The Family in Renaissance Florence*, trans. R. N. Watkins. Columbia, S. C.: University of South Carolina Press, 1969.

Aldhelm. "De laudibus virginitatis sive de virginate sanctorum," in *Patrologiae cursus completus*, ed. J. P. Migne. Paris, 1844-64. LXXXIX, 103-62.

———. "De laudibus virginum," in *Patrologiae cursus completus*, ed. J. P. Migne. Paris, 1844-64. LXXXIX, 237-80.

Ambrose. "Ad virginem devotam," in *Patrologiae cursus completus*, ed. J. P. Migne. Paris, 1845. XVII, 579-84.

———. "De virginibus ad Marcellinam sororem suam," in *Patrologiae cursus completus*, ed. J. P. Migne. Paris, 1845. XVI, 187-234.

———. "De institutione virginis," in *Patrologiae cursus completus*, ed. J. P. Migne. Paris, 1845. XVI, 305-34.

———. "De viduis," in *Patrologiae cursus completus*, ed. J. P. Migne. Paris, 1845. XVI, 233-62.

Aquinas, Thomas. *Basic Writings of Saint Thomas Aquinas*, ed. A. C. Pegis. New York: Random House, 1945.

Athanasius. "Exhortatio ad sponsam Christi," in *Patrologiae cursus completus*, ed. J. P. Migne. Paris, 1851. CIII, 671-84.

Augustine. "De bono viduitatis liber seu epistola ad Julianam viduam," in *Patrologiae cursus completus*, ed. J. P. Migne. Paris, 1845. XL, 429-50.

———. "De sancta virginitate," in *Patrologiae cursus completus*, ed. J. P. Migne. Paris, 1845. XL, 395-428.

————. *Select Letters*, ed. James H. Baxter. Cambridge, Mass.: Harvard University Press, 1965.

Avit. "De consolatoria laude castitatis ad Fuscinam sororem," in *Patrologiae cursus completus*, ed. J. P. Migne. Paris, 1844-64. LIX, 369-82.

Barberino, Francesco. *Del Reggimento e costumi di donna*, ed. Carlo Baudi di Vesme. *Collezione di opere inedite o rare dei primi tre secoli della lingua*. II. Bologna: Presso Gaetano Romagnoli, 1875.

Bartholomew Anglicus. *Mediaeval Lore from Bartholomew Anglicus*, ed. Robert Steele. London: Chatto & Windus, 1924.

Bartsch, Karl, ed. *Provenzalisches Lesebuch*. Elberfeld: R. L. Friderichs, 1855.

Boccaccio, Giovanni. *Concerning Famous Women*, trans. Guido A. Guarino. New Brunswick: Rutgers University Press, 1963.

Bogin, Meg, trans. *The Women Troubadours*. New York: Paddington Press, 1976.

Boileau, Etienne. *Le Livre des métiers d'Etienne Boileau*, eds. Rene de Lespinasse, François Bonnardot. Paris: Imprimerie Nationale, 1879.

Bornstein, Diane, ed. *Distaves and Dames: Renaissance Treatises For and About Women*. Delmar, N. Y.: Scholars' Facsimiles and Reprints, 1978.

Caesarius. "Regula ad virgines," in *Patrologiae cursus completus*, ed. J. P. Migne. Paris, 1844-64. LXVII, 1103-21.

————. "Ad Caesariam abbatissam ejusque congregationem," in *Patrologiae cursus completus*, ed. J. P. Migne. Paris, 1844-64. LXVII, 1125-35.

————. "Epistola hortatoria ad virginem Deo dedicatam," in *Patrologiae cursus completus*, ed. J. P. Migne. Paris, 1844-64. LXVII, 1135-38.

Capellanus, Andreas. *The Art of Courtly Love*, trans. John J. Parry. New York: Norton, 1969.

Castiglione, Baldassare. *The Book of the Courtier*, trans. Thomas Hoby. London: David Nutt, 1900.

Caxton, William, trans. *The Book of the Knight of the Tower*, ed. M. Y. Offord. London: EETS, 1971.

Chaucer, Geoffrey. *The Works of Geoffrey Chaucer*, ed. F. N. Robinson. Boston: Houghton Mifflin Co., 1957.

Chazaud, A. M., ed. *Les Enseignements d'Anne de France à sa fille Suzanne de Bourbon*. Moulins: C. Desrosiers, 1878.

Chrétien de Troyes. *Le Chevalier de la Charrette*, ed. Mario Roques. Paris: Champion, 1972.

Cockayne, Oswald, ed. *Hali Meidenhad*. London: EETS, 1866.

Constans, L., ed. "La Cour d'Amour," *Revue des Langues Romanes*, 3rd Series, 6 (1881), 157-79, 209-20, 261-76.

Cyprian. "De habitu virginum," in *Libri De Catholicae ecclesiae unitate. De lapsis, et De habitu virginum*, ed. J. G. Krabinger. Tübingen, 1853.

———. *The Treatises of S. Caecilius Cyprian*, trans. Charles Thornton. Oxford, 1840.

Davis, Norman, ed. *Paston Letters and Papers of the Fifteenth Century*. Oxford: Oxford University Press, 1971.

Day, Mabel, ed. *The English Text of the Ancrene Riwle Edited from Cotton Ms. Nero A XIV*. London: EETS, 1952.

Doutrepont, A., ed. *La Clef d'amors*. Halle: Max Niemeyer, 1890.

Durand de Champagne. *Le Miroir des dames*. Bibliothèque Nationale, fonds français 610.

———. *Speculum dominarum*. Bibliothèque Nationale, manuscrits latins 6784.

Erasmus, Desidirius. *The Praise of Folly*, trans. H. Hudson. Princeton: Princeton University Press [1941].

———. *The Education of a Christian Prince*, trans. Lester K. Born. New York: Columbia University Press, 1936.

Ermengaud, Matfre. *Le Breviari d'amor de Matfre Ermengaud*, ed. Peter T. Ricketts. Leiden: E. J. Brill, 1976.

Fougères, Etienne de. *Le Livre des manières par Etienne de Fougères*, ed. F. Talbert. Paris: Libraire du College de France, 1877.

Furnivall, F. J., ed. *A Booke of Precedence*. London: EETS, 1869.

———. *Early English Meals and Manners*. London: EETS, 1868; reprinted as *The Babees' Book*. New York: Greenwood Press, 1969.

Garin lo Brun. "L'Enseignement de Garin lo Brun," ed. Carl Appel. *Revue des Langues Romanes*, 33 (1889), 409-29.

Gori, Pietro, ed. *Dodici avvertimenti che deve dare la madre alla figliuola quando la manda a marito*. Florence: A. Salani, 1885.

Hoccleve, Thomas, trans. "Letter of Cupid," in *Hoccleve's Works*, ed. I. Gollancz. London: EETS, 1925.

Jean de Meun and Guillaume de Lorris. *The Romance of the Rose*, trans. Charles Dahlberg. Princeton: Princeton University Press, 1971.

Jerome. *Select Letters of Jerome*, ed. F. A. Wright. Cambridge, Mass.: Harvard University Press, 1963.

————. "Ad Demetriadem de servanda virginitate," in *Patrologiae cursus completus*, ed. J. P. Migne. Paris, 1845. XXII, 1107-24.

John of Salisbury. *The Statesman's Book of John of Salisbury*, trans. John Dickinson. New York: Alfred A. Knopf, 1927.

Kempe, Margery. *The Book of Margery Kempe*, eds. Sanford B. Meech, Hope Emily Allen. London: EETS, 1940.

Kingsford, C. L., ed. *The Stonor Letters and Papers*. London: Royal Historical Society, 1919.

Knust, Hermann, ed. "Castigos y dotrinas que un sabio dava a sus hijas," in *Dos obras didacticas y dos legendos sacadas de manuscritos de la Biblioteca del Escorial*. Madrid, 1878.

Körting, Gustav, ed. *L'Art d'amors und Li Remedes d'amors. Zwei altfranzösische Lehrgedicte von Jacques d'Amiens*. Leipzig, 1868.

La Tour-Landry, Geoffrey de. *Le Livre du chevalier de la Tour-Landry*, ed. A. Montaiglon. Paris: P. Jannet, 1854.

————. *The Book of the Knight of La Tour-Landry*, ed. Thomas Wright. London: EETS, 1868.

Leitzmann, Albert, ed. *König Tirol, Winsbeke und Winsbekin*. Halle: Max Niemeyer, 1888.

Loomis, R. S. and L. H. Loomis, eds. *Medieval Romances*. New York: Random House, 1957.

Louis, Saint. "Enseignements à sa fille Isabelle," in *Recueil des historiens des Gaules et de la France*, eds. Daunou, Naudet. Paris: Imprimerie Royale, 1840. vol. XX.

————. "Conseils de Saint Louis à une de ses filles," in *Recueil des historiens des Gaules et de la France*, eds. De Wailly, Delisle, Jourdain. Paris: Imprimerie Royale, 1840. vol. XXIII.

Migne, J. P., ed. *Patrologiae cursus completus*. Paris, 1844-64.

Mustanoja, Tauno, ed. *The Good Wife Taught Her Daughter. The Good Wyfe Wold a Pylgremage. The Thewis of Gud Women*. Helsinki, 1948.

Navarre, Philippe de. *Les Quatre âges de l'homme*, ed. Marcel de Freville. Paris: SATF, 1888.

Pichon, Jerome, ed. *Le Ménagier de Paris*. Paris: Crapelet, 1846.

Pizan, Christine de. *The Book of the Three Virtues*, trans. Charity C. Willard. Unpublished translation, 1975.

————. *Le Trésor de la Cité des dames selon dame Cristine.* Paris: Anthoine Verard, 1497.

————. *Le Livre des trois vertus.* Bibliothèque Nationale, fonds français 452.

————. [Du Castel]. *The Boke of the Cyte of Ladyes,* trans. B. Anslay. London: H. Pepwell, 1521.

————. *Le Livre de la Cité des dames.* Bibliothèque Nationale, fonds français 607. British Museum, Harley Ms. 4431, fols. 290-374.

————. *The Book of Fayttes of Armes and of Chyvalrye,* ed. A. T. P. Byles. London: EETS, 1932.

————. *The Middle English Translation of Christine de Pisan's Livre du corps de policie,* ed. Diane Bornstein. Heidelberg: Carl Winter, 1977.

————. *Le Livre du corps de policie,* ed. R. Lucas. Paris and Geneva: Librairie Droz, 1967.

————. *The Livre de la paix of Christine de Pisan,* ed. Charity C. Willard. The Hague: Mouton, 1958.

————. *Le Livre des fais et bonnes meurs du sage roy Charles V,* ed. Suzanne Solente. 2 vols. Paris: SATF, 1936, 1941.

————. *The Epistles of the Romance of the Rose and Other Documents in the Debate,* ed. Charles F. Ward. Chicago: University of Chicago, 1911.

————. *Lavision Christine,* ed. Sister Mary Louise Towner. Washington, D. C.: Catholic University, 1932.

————. *Le Livre de la Mutacion de Fortune,* ed. Suzanne Solente. Paris: SATF, 1959-66. 4 vols.

————. *Jeanne d'Arc, chronique rimée.* Orleans: H. Herluison, 1865.

————. *The Morale Proverbes of Christyne.* Westminster, 1478. Reprinted Amsterdam and New York: Da Capo Press, 1970.

————. *Oeuvres Poétiques de Christine de Pisan,* ed. Maurice Roy. Paris: SATF, 1891. 3 vols.

Power, Eileen, trans. *The Goodman of Paris.* New York: Harcourt, Brace & Co., 1928.

Rickert, Edith, trans. *The Babees' Book: Medieval Manners for the Young.* New York: Cooper Square Publishers, 1966.

Robert of Blois. *Robert von Blois sämtliche Werke,* ed. Jacob Ulrich. Berlin: Mayer & Muller, 1889.

Scrope, Stephen, trans. *The Epistle of Othea*, ed. Curt F. Bühler. London: EETS, 1970.

Sneyd, Charlotte A., trans. *A Relation or rather a True Account of the Island of England*. London: Camden Society, 1847.

Sordello. *Le Poesie inedite di Sordello*, ed. Giuseppe Palazzi. Venezia: Tipografia Antonelli, 1887.

Stapleton, T., ed. *The Plumpton Correspondence*. London: Camden Society, 1839.

Tertullian. "De monogamia," in *Patrologiae cursus completus*, ed. J. P. Migne. Paris, 1844. II, 929-54.

————. "De cultu feminarum," in *Patrologiae cursus completus*, ed. J. P. Migne. Paris, 1844. I, 1303-34.

————. "Ad uxorem," in *Patrologiae cursus completus*, ed. J. P. Migne. Paris, 1844. I, 1275-1304.

Vives, J. L. *A Very Frutefull and Pleasant Boke Called the Instruction of a Christen Woman*. London [1540].

SECONDARY SOURCES

Abram, A. *Social England in the Fifteenth Century*. London: G. Routledge, 1909.

————. *English Life and Manners in the Later Middle Ages*. London: G. Routledge, 1913.

————. "Women Traders in Medieval London," *Economic Journal*, 26 (1916), 276-85.

Ariès, Philippe. *Centuries of Childhood*, trans. Robert Baldick. New York: Knopf, 1962.

Bagley, J. J. *Margaret of Anjou, Queen of England*. London: Herbert Jenkins, 1948.

Bandel, Betty. "The English Chroniclers' Attitude toward Women," *Journal of the History of Ideas*, 16 (1955), 113-18.

Bardeche, Maurice. *Histoire des femmes*. Paris: Stock, 1968.

Beard, Mary. *Woman as a Force in History*. New York: Collier Books, 1962.

Beauvoir, Simone de. *The Second Sex*. New York: Vintage Books, 1952.

Bell, Susan G., ed. *Women from the Greeks to the French Revolution*. Belmont, California: Wadsworth Publishing, 1973.

Bennett, H. S. *The Pastons and their England*. Cambridge: Cambridge University Press, 1922; reprinted 1970.

————. *Life on the English Manor.* Cambridge: Cambridge University Press, 1938.

————. *Six Medieval Men and Women.* Cambridge: Cambridge University Press, 1955.

Benton, John F. "The Court of Champagne as a Literary Center," *Speculum*, 36 (1961), 551-91.

Bolton, Brenda M. "Mulieres Sanctae," in *Women in Medieval Society*, ed. Susan M. Stuard. Philadelphia: University of Pennsylvania Press, 1976.

Bornstein, Diane. *Mirrors of Courtesy.* Hamden, Connecticut: Archon Books, 1975.

————. "An Historical Survey of Women's Language: from Medieval Courtesy Books to Seventeen Magazine," in *Women's Language and Style*, eds. D. Butturff, E. L. Epstein. Akron, Ohio: L & S Books, 1978.

————. *Ideals for Women in the Works of Christine de Pizan.* Ann Arbor: Medieval Monographs, 1981.

————. "Women's Public and Private Space in Some Medieval Courtesy Books," *Centerpoint*, 3 (1981), 68-74.

Brion, Marcel. *Blanche de Castille, femme de Louis VIII, mère de Saint Louis.* Paris: Les Editions de France, 1939.

Brittain, Alfred. *Woman in All Ages and in All Countries.* Philadelphia: George Barrie & Sons, 1907.

Bullough, Vern L. *The Subordinate Sex.* Urbana, Illinois: University of Illinois Press, 1973.

Burckhardt, Jacob. *The Civilisation of the Period of the Renaissance in Italy.* London: C. Kegan Paul, 1878.

Butler, Pierce. *Women in All Ages and in All Countries: Women of Medieval France.* Philadelphia: George Barrie & Sons, 1907.

Calmette, Joseph. *The Golden Age of Burgundy.* New York: Norton, 1963.

Camden, Carroll. *The Elizabethan Woman.* New York: The Elsevier Press, 1952.

Campaux, Antoine. *La Question des femmes au xve siècle.* Paris, 1865.

Campbell, P. G. C. "Christine de Pisan en Angleterre," *Revue de Littérature Comparée*, 5 (1925), 659-70.

Carruthers, Mary. "The Wife of Bath and the Painting of Lions," *PMLA*, 94 (1979), 209-22.

Cartellieri, Otto. *The Court of Burgundy*. New York: Alfred A. Knopf, 1929.

Chojnacki, Stanley. "Dowries and Kinsmen in Early Renaissance Venice," in *Women in Medieval Society*, ed. Susan M. Stuard. Philadelphia: University of Pennsylvania, 1976.

Clephan, Robert C. *The Tournament: its Periods and Phases*. New York: Ungar Publishing, 1967.

Coleman, Emily. "Infanticide in the Early Middle Ages," in *Women in Medieval Society*, ed. Susan M. Stuard. Philadelphia: University of Pennsylvania, 1976.

Collis, Louise. *Memoirs of a Medieval Woman. The Life and Times of Margery Kempe*. New York: Crowell, 1964.

Coulton, G. G. *Medieval Panorama. The English Scene from Conquest to Reformation*. Cambridge: The University Press, 1944.

—————. *Life in the Middle Ages*. 4 vols. Cambridge: The University Press, 1928-30.

—————. *Social Life in Britain from the Conquest to the Reformation*. Cambridge: The University Press, 1918.

Crane, Thomas F. *Italian Social Customs of the Sixteenth Century and their Influence on the Literatures of Europe*. New Haven: Yale University Press, 1920.

Davis, Natalie Z. *Society and Culture in Early Modern France*. Stanford: Stanford University Press, 1975.

Defourneaux, Marcelin. *La Vie quotidienne au temps de Jeanne d'Arc*. Paris: Hachette, 1952.

Denomy, Alexander. "An Inquiry into the Origins of Courtly Love," *Medieval Studies*, 6 (1944), 175-260.

—————. "Courtly Love and Courtliness," *Speculum*, 28 (1953), 44-63.

Dillard, Heath. "Women in Reconquest Castile: The Fueros of Sepulveda and Cuenca," in *Women in Medieval Society*, ed. Susan M. Stuard. Philadelphia: University of Pennsylvania, 1976.

Donaldson, James. *Woman: Her Position and Influence in Ancient Greece and Rome and among the Early Christians*. New York: Gordon Press, 1973.

Duby, Georges. *Medieval Marriage*. Baltimore: Johns Hopkins University Press, 1978.

Du Castel, F. *Damoiselle Christine de Pisan, veuve de M. Etienne de Castel*. Paris: Picard, 1972.

Eckenstein, Lina. *Woman under Monasticism*. Cambridge: Cambridge University Press, 1896.

Einstein, Lewis. *The Italian Renaissance in England*. New York: Columbia University Press, 1935.

Facinger, Marion. "A Study of Medieval Queenship: Capetian France, 987-1237," *Studies in Medieval and Renaissance History*, 5 (1968), 1-47.

Fawtier, Robert. *The Capetian Kings of France*. London: Macmillan, 1960.

Ferrante, Joan M. *Woman as Image in Medieval Literature*. New York: Columbia University Press, 1975.

———— and George Economou, eds. *In Pursuit of Perfection: Courtly Love in Medieval Literature*. New York: Kennikat Press, 1975.

Firestone, Shulamith. *The Dialectic of Sex*. New York: Bantam Books, 1971.

Funck-Brentano, F. *The Middle Ages*. London: William Heinemann, 1922.

Gabriel, Asztrik L. "The Educational Ideas of Christine de Pisan," *Journal of the History of Ideas*, 16 (1955) 3-21.

Gies, Frances and Joseph. *Women in the Middle Ages*. New York: Barnes & Noble, 1980.

Gardiner, Dorothy. *English Girlhood at School. A Study of Women's Education through Twelve Centuries*. London: Oxford University Press, 1929.

Goodsell, Willystine. *A History of Marriage and the Family*. New York: Macmillan, 1935.

Green, Mary. *Lives of the Princesses of England*. 6 vols. London: H. Colburn, 1849-55.

Hanawalt, Barbara A. "The Female Felon in Fourteenth Century England," in *Women in Medieval Society*, ed. Susan M. Stuard. Philadelphia: University of Pennsylvania Press, 1976.

————. "The Peasant Family and Crime in Fourteenth Century England," *Journal of British Studies*, 13 (1974), 1-18.

Hanning, Robert W. "From *Eva* to *Ave* to Eglentyne and Alisoun: Chaucer's Insight into Roles Women Play," *Signs*, 2 (1977), 580-99.

Harksen, Sibylle. *Women in the Middle Ages*. New York: Abner Schram, 1975.

Haskins, Charles H. *The Renaissance of the Twelfth Century*. Cambridge, Mass.: Harvard University Press, 1928.

Healy, E. M. *Woman According to Saint Bonaventure*. New York: Georgian Press, 1955.

Heer, F. *The Medieval World, Europe 1100-1350*. New York: World Publishing Company, 1962.

Hentsch, Alice A. *De la littérature didactique du moyen âge s'adressant spécialement aux femmes*. Halle: Université de Halle-Wittenberg, 1903.

Herlihy, David. "Land, Family, and Women in Continental Europe, 701-1200," in *Women in Medieval Society*, ed. Susan M. Stuard. Philadelphia: University of Pennsylvania, 1976.

————. "Life Expectancies for Women in Medieval Society," in *The Role of Woman in the Middle Ages*. ed. Rosmarie T. Morewedge (Albany: State University of New York, 1975).

Hill, Georgiana. *Women in English Life*. London: R. Bentley & Son, 1896.

Hilton, Rodney. *Bond Men Made Free*. New York: Viking Press, 1973.

Hogrefe, Pearl. *Tudor Women: Commoners and Queens*. Ames, Iowa: Iowa State University Press, 1975.

————. *Women of Action in Tudor England*. Ames, Iowa: Iowa State University Press, 1977.

Holmes, Urban and J. R. Tigner. *Daily Living in the Twelfth Century based on the Observations of Alexander Neckam in London and Paris*. Madison, Wisconsin: University of Wisconsin Press, 1952.

Homans, George C. *English Villagers in the Thirteenth Century*. New York: Harper, 1970.

Howard, George E. *A History of Matrimonial Institutions*. 3 vols. Chicago: University of Chicago Press, 1904.

Hughes, Muriel Joy. *Women Healers in Medieval Life and Literature*. New York: King's Crown Press, 1943.

Huizinga, J. *The Waning of the Middle Ages*. London: Edward Arnold, 1927.

Kelly, Amy. *Eleanor of Aquitaine and the Four Kings*. Cambridge, Mass.: Harvard University Press, 1951.

————. "Eleanor of Aquitaine and her Courts of Love," *Speculum*, 12 (1937), 3-19.

Kelly, Henry A. *Love and Marriage in the Age of Chaucer*. Ithaca: Cornell University Press, 1975.

Kelso, Ruth. *Doctrine for the Lady of the Renaissance*. Urbana, Ill.: University of Illinois Press, 1956.

————. *The Doctrine of the English Gentleman in the Sixteenth Century*. Urbana, Ill.: University of Illinois Press, 1929.

Labarge, Margaret Wade. *A Baronial Household of the Thirteenth Century*. New York: Barnes & Noble, 1965.

Lafitte-Houssat, J. *Troubadours et cours d'amour*. Paris: Presses Universitaires de France, 1950.

Laigle, Mathilde. *Le Livre des trois vertus*. Paris: Champion, 1912.

Lakoff, Robin. *Language and Woman's Place*. New York: Harper, 1975.

Laslett, P. and R. Wall. *Household and Family in Past Time*. Cambridge: The University Press, 1972.

Le Gentil, Pierre. "Christine de Pisan, poète méconnu," in *Mélanges Daniel Mornet*. Paris: Nizet, 1951.

Lehmann, André. *Le Rôle de la femme dans l'histoire de France au moyen âge*. Paris: Berger-Levrault, 1952.

Lewis, Archibald. *The Development of Southern French and Catalan Society*: Austin: University of Texas Press, 1965.

Lewis, C. S. *The Allegory of Love*. London: Oxford University Press, 1948.

McCash, June Hall Martin. "Marie de Champagne and Eleanor of Aquitaine: a Relationship Re-examined," *Speculum*, 54 (1979), 698-711.

McDonnel, Ernest W. *The Beguines and Beghards in Medieval Culture with Special Emphasis on the Belgian Scene*. New Brunswick, N.J.: Rutgers University Press, 1954.

McGibbon, David. *Elizabeth Woodville, her Life and Times*. London: Arnold Baker, 1938.

McLeod, Enid. *The Order of the Rose: the Life and Ideas of Christine de Pisan*. Totowa, N. J.: Rowman & Littlefield, 1976.

McNamara, Jo-ann and Suzanne F. Wemple, "Marriage and Divorce in the Frankish Kingdom," in *Women in Medieval Society*, ed. Susan M. Stuard. Philadelphia: University of Pennsylvania, 1976.

Malinowski, B. *Sex, Culture and Myth*. New York: Harcourt, 1962.

Malvern, Marjorie. *Venus in Sackcloth*. Carbondale, Ill.: Southern Illinois University Press, 1975.

Mason, John E. *Gentlefolk in the Making*. Philadelphia: University of Pennsylvania Press, 1935.

Matthews, William. "The Wife of Bath and All Her Sect," *Viator*, 5 (1974), 413-43.

Maulde la Claviere, R. de. *The Women of the Renaissance: a Study of Feminism*. London: Swan Sonnenschein & Co., 1900.

Miller, Casey and Kate Swift. *Words and Women*. New York: Doubleday, 1976.

Miller, Robert P. "The Wounded Heart: Courtly Love and the Medieval Antifeminist Tradition," *Women's Studies*, 2 (1974), 335-50.

Millet, Fred B. "English Courtesy Literature before 1557," *Bulletin of the Department of History and Economic Science*, 30 (Ontario: Queens University, 1919).

Mohl, Ruth. *The Three Estates in Medieval and Renaissance Literature*. New York: Columbia University Press, 1933.

Moller, Herbert. "The Social Causation of the Courtly Love Complex," *Comparative Studies in Society and History*, 1 (1958), 147-63.

Morewedge, Rosmarie T., ed. *The Role of Woman in the Middle Ages*. Albany: State University of New York Press, 1975.

Newman, F. X., ed. *The Meaning of Courtly Love*. Albany: State University of New York, 1968.

Oberembt, Kenneth. "Chaucer's Anti-Misogynist Wife of Bath," *Chaucer Review*, 10 (1976), 287-302.

O'Faolain, Julia and Lauro Martines. *Not in God's Image*. New York: Harper, 1973.

Owst, G. R. *Literature and Pulpit in Medieval England*. Oxford: Oxford University Press, 1961.

Painter, Sidney. *French Chivalry*. Baltimore: The Johns Hopkins Press, 1940.

Pelicier, Paul. *Essai sur le gouvernement de la Dame de Beaujeu*. Chartres, 1882. Reprinted Geneva: Slatkine Reprints, 1970.

Phillips, M. and W. S. Tomkinson. *English Women in Life and Letters*. London, 1926. Reprinted New York: Benjamin Blom, 1971.

Phillpots, Bertha. *Kindred and Clan in the Middle Ages and After.* Cambridge: The University Press, 1913.

Piaget, Arthur. "Un Manuscrit de la Cour Amoureuse de Charles VI," *Romania,* 31 (1902), 597-603.

Pinet, Marie Josephe. *Christine de Pisan, 1364-1430.* Paris: Champion, 1927.

Pomeroy, Sarah B. *Goddesses, Whores, Wives and Slaves.* New York: Schocken Books, 1975.

Powell, C. L. *English Domestic Relations, 1487-1653.* New York: Columbia University Press, 1917.

Power, Eileen. *Medieval Women.* Cambridge: The University Press, 1975.

————. *Medieval People.* New York: Barnes & Noble, 1963.

————. *Medieval Nunneries.* Cambridge: The University Press, 1922.

————. "The Position of Women," in *The Legacy of the Middle Ages,* eds. C. G. Crump and E. F. Jacob. Oxford: Oxford University Press, 1926.

Putnam, Emily. *The Lady.* New York: G. P. Putnam, 1919.

Quennell, M. *A History of Everyday Things in England.* New York: Scribner, 1920.

Reeves, Marjorie. *The Medieval Village.* London: Longmans, 1959.

Reiss, Edmund. "Fin' Amors: Its History and Meaning in Medieval Literature," *Journal of Medieval and Renaissance Studies,* 8 (1979), 74-99.

Richardson, Lula M. *The Forerunners of Feminism in French Literature of the Renaissance from Christine of Pisa to Marie de Gournay.* Baltimore: The Johns Hopkins Press, 1929.

Riencourt, Amaury de. *Sex and Power in History.* New York: David McKay, 1974.

Rogers, Katherine M. *The Troublesome Helpmate: a History of Misogyny in Literature.* Seattle: University of Washington Press, 1966.

Rowbotham, John F. *The Troubadours and Courts of Love.* London and New York: Macmillan, 1895.

Schoenfeld, H. *Women in All Ages and in All Countries: Women of the Teutonic Nations.* Philadelphia: George Barrie & Sons, 1907.

Seltman, Charles. *Women in Antiquity.* London and New York: Thames & Hudson, 1956.

Stenton, Doris. *The English Woman in History*. London: George Allen & Unwin, 1957.

Stenton, F. M. "The Place of Women in Anglo-Saxon Society," *Royal Historical Society, Transactions*, 25 (1943).

Stone, Lawrence. *The Family, Sex and Marriage in England, 1500-1800*. New York: Harper & Row, 1977.

Strayer, Joseph. *The Reign of Philip the Fair*. Princeton: Princeton University Press, 1980.

Stuard, Susan M. "Women in Charter and Statute Law: Medieval Ragusa/Dubrovnik," in *Women in Medieval Society*, ed. Susan M. Stuard. Philadelphia: University of Pennsylvania Press, 1976.

Sullerot, Evelyne. *Woman, Society and Change*. New York: McGraw Hill, 1971.

————. *Histoire et sociologie du travail feminin*. Paris: Gonthier, 1968.

Tavard, George H. *Woman in Christian Tradition*. Notre Dame: University of Notre Dame Press, 1973.

Thompson, J. W. *The Literacy of the Laity in the Middle Ages*. New York: B. Franklin, 1960.

Thorne, Barrie and Nancy Henley, eds. *Language and Sex*. Rowley, Mass.: Newbury House, 1975.

Thrupp, Sylvia L. *The Merchant Class of Medieval London*. Ann Arbor: University of Michigan, 1948.

————. "The Problem of Conservatism in the Fifteenth Century," *Speculum*, 18 (1943), 363-68.

Tobin, Rosemary B. "Vincent of Beauvais on the Education of Women," *Journal of the History of Ideas*, 35 (1974), 485-89.

Topsfield, L. T. *Troubadours and Love*. Cambridge: The University Press, 1975.

Trevelyan, G. M. *English Social History: a Survey of Six Centuries, Chaucer to Queen Victoria*. London: Longmans, 1942.

Utley, Francis L. *The Crooked Rib*. Ohio: Ohio State University Press, 1944; reprinted New York: Octagon Books, 1970.

Walker, Curtis Howe. *Eleanor of Aquitaine*. Richmond: University of North Carolina Press, 1950.

Walker, Sue Sheridan. "Widow and Ward: The Feudal Law of Child Custody in Medieval England," in *Women in Medieval Society*, ed. Susan M. Stuard. Philadelphia: University of Pennsylvania Press, 1976.

Watson, Foster. *Vives and the Renaissance Education of Women*. London: Edward Arnold, 1912.

Welch, Alice Kemp. *Of Six Medieval Women*. London: Macmillan, 1913.

Willard, Charity C. "The Manuscript Tradition of the *Livre des trois vertus* and Christine de Pisan's Audience," *Journal of the History of Ideas*, 27 (1966), 433-44.

————. "A Fifteenth Century View of Women's Role in Medieval Society: Christine de Pisan's *Livre des trois vertus*," in *The Role of Woman in the Middle Ages*, ed. Rosmarie T. Morewedge. Albany: State University of New York Press, 1975.

————. "Christine de Pizan: the Astrologer's Daughter," in *Mélanges à la memoire de Franco Simone*, I. Geneva: Slatkine, 1980.

Wright, Thomas. *A History of Domestic Manners and Sentiments in England*. London: Chapman & Hall, 1863.

————. *Womankind in Western Europe from the Earliest Times till the xvii Century*. London: Groombridge & Sons, 1869.

Zinserling, Verena. *Women in Greece and Rome*. New York: Abner Schram, 1972.

Index

151